16.95

MICHIGAN WILDFLOWERS IN COLOR

D1550597

DATE DUE		
NOV 2 8 1997		
DEC 1 9 1997 JAN 2 7 1998		
APR 1 4 1998		
MAY 1 8 1998		
AUG 0 5 1998		
OCT 0 7 1999		
NOV 2 8 1999		
MAY 3 0 2000		
MAY 1 5 2001		
GAYLORD		PRINTED IN U.S.A

Published by: Northmont Publishing, Inc.
  6346 Orchard Lake Road
  West Bloomfield, Michigan
  48322

Library of Congress Catalog Card
  Number: 85-90152

ISBN: 0-9614818-0-3

First Printing 1985 Copyright 1985
Second, Revised Printing 1988 Copyright 1988
Third Printing 1991 Copyright 1991
Fourth Printing 1992 Copyright 1992
Fifth Printing 1993 Copyright 1993
Sixth Printing 1994 Copyright 1994

Printed in the U.S.A.

Michigan Wildflowers

IN COLOR

Harry C. Lund

Author and photographer

Northmont Publishing, Inc.
West Bloomfield, Michigan

Foreword

Education is the lantern of the soul.
How fortunate we in Michigan are to
have writers able to produce a book that
opens new avenues of learning to
children, students, and adults.

The author has spent innumerable days,
weeks, and months in search of his
subject matter. Flowers have their own
time of emergence often in such
simultaneous numbers, and of such
duration of bloom that years are
involved to capture them all photo-
graphically. This book is easy enough
for any layman to understand and yet is
complete enough in nomenclature to
whet the appetite of anyone who has
ever wanted to know the name of a
wildflower.

This book is the meeting of Michigan's
wealth of nature with the searching
minds of lovers of the outdoors.
Through it may you become more aware
of the great need to protect our rich
heritage of beauty in Michigan.

Mrs. William B. Heermann (Erie),
    President
The Federated Garden Clubs of
    Michigan, Inc.
1983-1985

Introduction

Experience with a former book, "Wildflowers of Sleeping Bear", indicated that people enjoy wildflower identification by means of color illustrations. It also made clear that a publication of this kind with a broader coverage will fill an often expressed need. Thus, this attempt to present the most common, most interesting, and most visible wildflowers in the State of Michigan is an answer to this need. With but few exceptions this publication covers herbaceous, or non-woody type of vegetation commonly thought of as wildflowers. It does include a few shrubs and vines that are so showy as to demand inclusion. Also included are plants often thought of as weeds.

Even though 278 species of wildflowers are represented here, it is certain that specimens will be encountered that are not illustrated. In a work of this kind it is a major task to decide which species to include because, unfortunately, a line does have to be drawn. From my own experience there is nothing more frustrating than to find, after much searching, that the flower at hand is not included in the book you have. As with all before me who have written books of this kind, I am sincerely sorry that this has to happen.

Anyone interested in wildflower identification is urged to have and use a good magnifying glass. A hand lens of 10 power magnification is small, inexpensive, convenient, and will not only aid in discerning distinguishing characteristics of plants but will open up a whole new exciting and interesting world.

As a very general help to identification a VISIBILITY RATING INDEX is used. A capital letter at each illustration indicates the visibility rating (see *Visibility Rating Key*). While not precise and very much dependent on the season of the year, the general weather conditions, and the location within the State, it is hoped that the system will be of help, especially in easily locating flowers that form great masses along our roadways.

As everyone recognizes, there are wildflowers that need the help of all of us to keep from vanishing from our heritage. Those with legal protection under the old "Michigan Christmas tree law" are not to be picked or disturbed without written permission of the landowner and are designated in this book as **A PROTECTED MICHIGAN WILDFLOWER – DO NOT DISTURB.** Legal protection is also assured some species under the Endangered Species Act of 1974 that provides that a list be made of species that are determined to be in danger of extinction throughout all or a significant part of their range. None of the plants covered in this book fall in the Endangered category at this time. However, this same Act provides protection for species that could possibly become Endangered. These plants are referred to in this book as **A THREATENED SPECIES DO NOT DISTURB.** No plant on either the Endangered Species list or the Threatened Species list is to be disturbed in any way without a complex legal procedure. Finally, the Michigan Department of Natural Resources has requested that some plants whose continued existence is precarious but have no legal protection not be picked. These plants carry the request in this book **PLEASE DO NOT PICK.** Of, course, wildflowers growing on State or National Park lands, Nature Reserves, and other designated areas are not be disturbed under any circumstances.

To my wife, Eloise Eckerman Lund my sincere Thanks for all her help and support!

So, as the "Birders" say to each other, "Good Birding". I say to you

Good Bloomin'!

5

Format

The basic organization of flowers in this book is within one of six color groupings; white, yellow and orange, pink to red, lavender to purple, blue, or green and brown. Within each color group attempt is made to follow a seasonal sequence with early blooming flowers preceding those coming later. Beyond this basic framework, flowers that are botanically related or with similarities are placed together where possible.

Each plant description contains the following information in this order:

Most recognized common name in this area. Where a second commonly accepted name is also popularly used, it, too, is given.

Technical genus and species name.

Common family name.

Technical family name.

Habitat(s) where most commonly found.

Season of bloom.

Height of plant at blossom time.

Flower description.

Leaf description.

Stem description, if needed for identification.

Description of the fruit, particularly if the fruit is a berry or is berry-like. Also, when known, an indication of the fruit's toxicity or edibility.

Whether the plant grows in groups (colonies).

An indication as to whether the plant has legal protection as a **PROTECTED MICHIGAN WILDFLOWER,** as an **ENDANGERED or THREATENED SPECIES,** or the informal (non-legal) protection requested by the Michigan Department of Natural Resources.

Habitats

The habitat, or environment, preferred by a plant is placed in one or more of the following:

woods: areas of hardwood (deciduous) trees consisting primarily of beech, birch, soft maple, hard maple, ash, or basswood, including the edges of these wooded areas. Wildflowers occuring here are usually the early spring blooming types found before the trees are in full leaf.

dry woods: predominant tree species are aspen (popple) and oak representing the deciduous trees and various coniferous (evergreen) trees including white, jack, and red pine. Bracken ferns are commonly found.

wet woods: stands of mostly coniferous trees such as black spruce and balsam fir growing on moist sites, and having ground cover of sphagnum and other mosses, ferns, and liverworts. Most common in the northern part of the State.

dunes: sandy areas of sparse and scattered vegetation bordering the Great Lakes, particularly the east shore of Lake Michigan. Also includes inland areas of similar characteristics formed on glacier deposited sands or ancient sandy beach ridges. Typical vegetation is juniper, beach grass, scattered pines, sand cherry and other shrubs.

meadows: As used in this book includes most open areas with (usually) no or very scattered tree or shrub growth and includes abandoned farm fields, fence rows, roadsides, ditch-banks, waste areas, and even clearings in the woods. May be dry or moist.

swamps: low area with a high water table so there is usually standing stagnant water. Tree growth is primarily white cedar that creates dense shade.

bogs: wet areas of densely matted vegetation formed of various sedges and other water tolerant plants and their decaying parts floating on the edges of some lakes and ponds or adjacent to them. As one walks on these mats they tend to sag and undulate. Their instability requires extreme care on the part of anyone walking on them.

swales: depressions in the terrain, usually limited in area, and wet or moist most of the year. Also includes river and stream bottomlands where pools and puddles are found in the spring.

aquatic: permanently wet areas such as ponds, lakes, and slow flowing streams.

shores: rocky, gravelly, or sandy beaches, particularly those of the Great Lakes but does include inland lakes.

Visibility Ratings:

A capital letter symbol is found adjacent to each illustration. For flowers that are not illustrated the letter is found in the Summary List in the back of the book. The letters have the following meanings:

A Conspicious flowers readily visible from a moving vehicle at normal highway driving speed. Usually create extensive masses of color.

B Distinctive flowers easily visible from a moving vehicle at normal highway driving speed but very seldom forming extensive masses of color.

C Showy flowers that are harder to find, either because of the nature of the blossoms, the plants are less frequent, or because of where they grow. Visible mainly along trails and off-road situations.

D Inconspicuous flowers visible to the careful observer.

Nomenclature:

The scientific names used are from the Manual of Vascular Plants of Northeastern United States and Adjacent Canada by Henry A. Gleason and Arthur Cronquist, 1963.

visibility rating	spring	summer	fall	white	yellow-orange	pink-red	lavender-purple	blue	green-brown	GUIDE — What, Where, When — Alphabetically by popular common name — Flowers WHITE or predominently WHITE	page	woods	dry woods	wet woods	dunes	meadows	swamps	bogs	swales	aquatic	shores
C	•	•		•						Alyssum, Hoary	44		•			•					
B	•	•		•						Anemone, Canada	28					•			•		
C	•			•		•				Anemone, Rue & False	30	•									
C	•			•		•				Anemone, Wood	28	•									
D	•			•		•				Arbutus, Trailing	28		•								
C		•		•						Asphodel, Sticky False	36							•	•		•
C		•		•						Aster, Flat-topped	52					•			•		
D		•		•						Baneberry, Red	40	•									
D		•		•						Baneberry, White	40	•									
C	•	•		•		•				Bearberry	34				•						
C		•		•		•				Bindweed, Field	44				•	•					
C	•			•						Bloodroot	26	•				•		•	•		
B		•	•	•			•			Boneset	50					•		•	•		
D	•	•		•	•		•			Broom-rape, Clustered	34				•						
D	•	•		•		•				Buckbean	34						•	•		•	
C	•	•		•						Bunchberry	28	•		•				•			
A	•	•		•						Campion, Bladder	36					•					
C		•	•	•						Campion, White	50					•					
A		•	•	•						Carrot, Wild	44					•					
C	•	•	•	•			•	•		Catnip	32					•					
C		•	•	•						Chamomile, Scentless	38					•					
D	•	•		•						Cinquefoil, Three-toothed	36										•
C		•		•						Comandra, Northern	40		•						•		•
D		•		•						Cow Wheat	48	•							•		•
C		•	•	•						Cucumber, Wild	52	•								•	
B		•		•			•			Culver's Root	48					•					
A		•		•						Daisy, Ox-eye	42					•					
C	•	•	•	•						Dogfennel	38					•					
C	•			•						Dutchman's Breeches	26	•									
A		•		•						Everlasting, Pearly	42					•					
A	•	•	•	•		•				Fleabane	36					•					
C	•			•						Foamflower	26	•									
D	•			•						Ginseng, Dwarf	32	•				•					
D	•			•						Goldthread	24			•				•	•		
C		•	•	•						Grass-of-Parnassus	52					•	•	•	•		•
C	•	•		•						Grass-of-Parnassus, Small	52					•	•	•	•		•
D	•	•		•					•	Greenbrier	34			•						•	
C		•	•	•						Hemlock, Water-	44						•	•			
D		•	•	•						Indian Pipe	48	•						•			
C		•		•				•		Indigo, Prairie False	38	•				•					

visibility rating	season of bloom			flower color						Guide (cont.) Flowers WHITE or predominantly WHITE (cont.)	page	habitats									
	spring	summer	fall	white	yellow-orange	pink-red	lavender-purple	blue	green-brown			woods	dry woods	wet woods	dunes	meadows	swamps	bogs	swales	aquatic	shores
D		•	•	•						Ladies'-tresses, Common	50					•		•	•		
C		•	•	•	•				•	Lettuce, White	52	•									
D		•		•						Lily, Dune	44				•						•
D	•			•						Lily, Fawn	54	•							•		•
C	•			•						Lily-of-the-valley, Wild	26	•							•		
B		•		•		•				Mallow, Musk	82					•					
C	•			•						May Apple	30	•									
A		•		•					•	Meadow-rue, Purple	42					•	•		•		•
B		•		•		•				Meadowsweet	40					•			•		
C	•			•						Mitrewort	24	•									
D	•	•		•						Mitrewort, Naked	24						•	•			
C		•	•	•	•		•			Mullein, Moth	40					•					
C		•		•						Nightshade, Enchanter's	34	•									
C		•		•	•					Painted Cup, Pale	48	•									•
B		•		•						Parsnip, Cow	44					•			•		
C		•		•						Parsnip, Water	46					•	•		•		
D		•		•						Partridgeberry	42	•	•								
D		•		•						Poison Ivy	48	•	•		•	•					
D	•			•		•	•			Primrose, Birdseye	28										•
C	•	•		•						Rock Cress, Lyre-leaved	32					•					•
C		•		•						Sandwort, Rock	38				•						•
D	•			•						Sarsaparilla	32	•									
D		•		•						Sarsaparilla, Bristly	32		•		•						
C		•		•						Shinleaf	46	•									
D		•		•					•	Shinleaf, Green	46		•								
D		•		•					•	Sidebells	46	•						•			
D	•	•		•						Snakeroot, Black	36	•									
C		•	•	•						Snakeroot, White	42	•									
C	•	•		•						Solomon's Seal, False	38	•									
D	•	•		•						Solomon's Seal, Hairy	38	•									
D	•	•		•						Solomon's Seal, Smooth	38	•									
C	•	•		•						Solomon's Seal, Starry False	38	•			•						
C	•			•						Spring Cress	24	•							•		
B		•	•	•						Spurge, Flowering	32		•			•					
C	•			•						Squirrel Corn	26	•									
C	•	•		•						Starflower	26	•						•	•		
D	•			•						Starwort	34		•		•						
D	•			•						Stichwort, Lesser	34	•				•					
C	•	•		•						Strawberry, Wild	36					•					
D	•	•		•						Strawberry, Woodland	36	•				•					

9

visibility rating	spring	summer	fall	white	yellow-orange	pink-red	lavender-purple	blue	green-brown	Guide (cont.)	page	woods	dry woods	wet woods	dunes	meadows	swamps	bogs	swales	aquatic	shores
										Flowers WHITE or predominently WHITE (cont.)											
D		•		•		•				Sundew, Round-leaved	50						•	•			
D	•			•						Sweet Cicely	30	•									
B		•		•						Thimbleberry	40	•				•					
D	•	•	•	•	•					Thistle, Pitcher's	32				•						
C	•	•		•						Toadflax, Bastard	40		•			•					
C	•			•		•				Toothwort, Broadleaf	24	•							•		
C	•			•		•				Toothwort, Cutleaf	24	•							•		
B	•			•		•				Trillium	30	•									
D	•	•		•						Trillium, Nodding	30	•									
B		•	•	•		•	•			Turtlehead	48					•			•		
C	•	•		•			•	•		Violet, Canada	30	•									
B		•	•	•						Virgin's Bower	52	•							•		
C	•			•						Water Arum	28						•	•		•	
D		•	•	•						Water-horehound, Cut-leaf	50						•		•		
B		•		•						Water Lily, White	50									•	
D		•		•						Wintergreen	46		•								
D		•		•		•				Woodnymph	46						•	•	•		
A		•	•	•		•				Yarrow	52					•					
										Flowers YELLOW and ORANGE											
C		•			•					Agrimony	66	•	•			•			•		
C	•				•					Bellwort, Large-flowered	54	•									
A		•	•		•					Birdsfoot Trefoil	68					•					
A		•	•		•					Black-eyed Susan	64					•					
A		•	•		•					Butter-and-eggs	68					•					
B	•	•	•		•					Buttercup	54					•	•		•		
B		•	•		•	•				Butterfly Weed	62				•	•					
C		•	•		•					Cherry, Ground	68					•					
B		•			•					Cinquefoil, Sulfur	64					•					
C	•	•			•					Clintonia	54	•						•			
B		•	•		•					Coneflower, Tall	70					•	•				
A	•	•			•					Coreopsis	56		•		•	•					
D	•				•					Cucumber-root, Indian	54	•									
A	•	•	•		•					Dandelion, Common	56					•					
B		•	•		•		•			Goat's-beard	62					•					
C		•			•	•				Goat's Rue	56		•			•					
C	•	•			•					Golden Alexanders	60					•			•		
C		•	•		•					Goldenrod, Bluestem	70	•	•			•					•
A		•	•		•					Goldenrod, Canada	70					•					

10

visibility rating	spring	summer	fall	white	yellow-orange	pink-red	lavender-purple	blue	green-brown	Guide (cont.) — Flowers YELLOW and ORANGE (Cont.)	page	woods	dry woods	wet woods	dunes	meadows	swamps	bogs	swales	aquatic	shores
A	•	•			•					Hawkweed, Field or Yellow	60					•					
A		•	•		•	•				Hawkweed, Orange	64					•					
A		•			•					Hawkweed, Smoothish	60					•					
C	•	•			•					Heather, False	58				•						
D		•	•	•	•		•			Horsemint	68					•	•				
C		•	•		•					Jewelweed, Spotted	64					•				•	
C		•			•					King Devil	60					•					
C	•				•					Lady's-slipper, Yellow	58			•			•	•			
B	•	•			•					Lily, Day	62					•			•		
B		•			•	•				Lily, Michigan	62					•			•		
B		•			•	•				Lily, Wood	62				•	•					
C	•				•					Lily, Yellow Trout	54	•		•		•			•		
D	•	•			•					Loosestrife, Tufted	56					•			•		
B	•				•					Marsh Marigold	54						•		•	•	
D	•				•		•			Meadow-rue, Early	42	•							•		
D		•			•					Moneywort	64					•			•		
B		•	•		•					Mullein, Common	68					•					
A	•	•	•		•					Parsnip, Wild	60					•					
D	•				•					Pimpernel, Yellow	60	•				•					
D		•	•		•	•			•	Pinesap	68	•									
B		•			•					Pondlily, Yellow	66									•	
B		•	•		•					Primrose, Evening	66		•		•	•					
C	•	•			•					Puccoon, Hairy	58		•		•	•					•
C	•	•			•					Puccoon, Hoary	58		•		•	•					•
B	•	•			•					Ragwort, Golden	56						•		•		
A		•	•		•					St. John's-wort, Common	66					•	•		•		•
C		•			•					Silverweed	64					•					•
B		•	•		•					Sowthistle, Smooth	66					•					
B	•	•	•		•					Spurge, Leafy	62				•	•					
D	•				•					Squawroot	58		•								
B		•	•		•					Sunflower, Tall	70					•	•				
B		•	•		•					Sunflower, Woodland	70	•				•			•		
B		•	•		•					Swamp Candle	66			•		•	•		•		
A		•	•		•					Tansy, Common	70					•					
C		•			•					Tansy, Huron	70				•				•		•
C	•		•		•					Violet, Downy Yellow	56	•									
C	•		•		•					Violet, Smooth Yellow	56	•									
C	•				•	•				Wood Betony	58	•	•								
C	•	•	•		•					Wood-sorrel, Yellow	58					•					
A	•	•			•					Yellow Rocket	60					•					

Guide (cont.)

Flowers PINK and RED

Visibility rating	spring	summer	fall	white	yellow-orange	pink-red	lavender-purple	blue	green-brown	Name	page	woods	dry woods	wet woods	dunes	meadows	swamps	bogs	swales	aquatic	shores
D	●	●				●				Arethusa	75						●	●			
C		●	●			●	●			Basil, Wild	82	●				●					
B		●				●	●			Bergamot, Wild	82					●					
B		●	●	●		●				Bouncing Bet	86					●					
D		●	●			●	●			Calypso	74			●		●					
B		●	●	●		●				Cardinal-flower	88					●			●		
B	●	●	●			●				Clover, Red	80					●					
C	●	●				●				Columbine	72	●	●			●			●		
C		●				●				Corn Cockle	86					●					
D	●	●	●			●				Corydalis, Pale	76					●					●
D		●				●				Cranberry, Large	80						●	●			
D		●				●				Cranberry, Small	80						●	●			
B	●	●		●		●	●			Dame's Rocket	82	●				●					
C		●		●		●				Dogbane, Spreading	84	●	●			●			●		
A		●	●			●	●			Fireweed	84					●			●		●
C	●	●		●		●			●	Geranium, Wild	76	●				●			●		
C		●		●		●	●			Grass Pink	78					●	●	●			
C	●			●		●	●	●		Hepatica, Round-lobed	72	●	●								
C	●			●		●				Hepatica, Sharp-lobed	72	●	●								
C	●	●				●				Herb-Robert	76	●				●			●		
C	●			●		●	●			Honesty	82	●				●					
A		●	●			●	●			Joe Pye Weed	88						●	●			●
C		●	●			●	●			Knapweed, Brown	88					●					
A		●	●	●		●	●			Knapweed, Spotted	88					●					
C	●	●				●				Lady's-slipper, Pink	74		●				●	●			
D	●			●		●	●			Lady's-slipper, Ram's-head	74	●		●			●	●			●
C		●		●		●				Lady's-slipper, Showy	78			●			●	●			
B		●		●		●				Mallow, Musk	82					●					
B		●				●	●			Milkweed, Common	84				●	●					
B		●		●		●	●			Milkweed, Swamp	84					●	●	●	●		
C		●		●		●	●		●	Milkwort, Field	84					●	●	●			
C		●		●		●				Milkwort, Racemed	78		●			●					
C		●		●		●				Mullein-pink	86					●					
D	●			●		●	●			Orchis, Showy	74	●				●					
B	●	●	●		●	●				Paintbrush, Indian	72					●					●
C		●				●	●			Pea, Beach	80				●						●
A	●	●		●		●	●			Pea, Everlasting	78					●					
C		●				●				Pink, Deptford	86					●					
D		●		●		●				Pipsissewa	80		●								
C	●	●				●				Pitcher Plant	76						●	●			●

visibility rating	spring	summer	fall	white	yellow-orange	pink-red	lavender-purple	blue	green-brown	Guide (cont.) Flowers PINK and RED (Cont.)	page	woods	dry woods	wet woods	dunes	meadows	swamps	bogs	swales	aquatic	shores
D		•				•				Pogonia, Rose	74					•		•			
C	•	•				•	•			Polygala, Fringed	78	•						•			
D		•				•	•			Pyrola, Pink	80	•						•			
C		•				•				Rose, Smooth	86	•			•	•					
C		•				•				Rose, Swamp	86						•	•	•		
C		•		•		•				Sleepy Catchfly	86		•			•					
C	•					•				Spring Beauty	72	•									
C	•					•				Spring Beauty, Broadleaf	72	•									
B		•	•	•		•	•			Teasel	84					•			•		
B		•	•			•	•			Thistle, Bull	88					•					
B		•	•	•		•	•			Thistle, Canada	88					•			•		
D		•				•	•			Thyme, Wild	82		•			•					•
C		•				•	•			Tick-trefoil, Pointed Leaved	94		•								
C	•			•	•	•	•		•	Trillium, Red	76	•									
D		•				•				Twinflower	78		•	•				•	•		
D	•	•				•	•			Twisted-stalk, Rose	76	•									
D	•	•		•		•	•			Twisted-stalk, White	76	•									
B		•		•		•				Vetch, Crown	80					•					
D	•	•		•	•	•	•			Windflower, Red	72				•						

Flowers LAVENDER to PURPLE

visibility rating	spring	summer	fall	white	yellow-orange	pink-red	lavender-purple	blue	green-brown	Guide (cont.)	page	woods	dry woods	wet woods	dunes	meadows	swamps	bogs	swales	aquatic	shores
C		•		•			•			Aster, Large-leaved	94	•	•								
B		•	•	•			•	•		Aster, New England	94					•			•		
B		•	•	•			•	•		Aster, Smooth	94				•	•					
C		•					•			Beard-tongue, Hairy	96	•				•					
B		•				•	•			Blazing Star, Rough	94					•					
C		•	•			•	•			Burdock, Common	94					•					
C		•	•			•	•			Burdock, Great	94					•					
C		•					•			Butterwort	92							•			•
C		•					•			Cinquefoil, Marsh	96						•	•	•	•	
D	•				•		•		•	Cohosh, Blue	90	•									
D	•			•	•					Coralroot, Northern or Early	92			•		•					
C		•				•	•			Coralroot, Spotted	92	•	•								
C	•	•				•	•			Coralroot, Striped	92	•	•	•							
D	•					•	•		•	Ginger, Wild	90	•									
C		•	•				•			Goat's-beard, Purple	62					•				•	
C		•				•	•			Hound's Tongue	92				•	•					
D	•					•	•		•	Jack-in-the-pulpit	90	•						•	•		
A		•	•				•			Loosestrife, Purple	96					•	•			•	•

visibility rating	season of bloom			flower color						Guide (cont.)	page	habitats									
	spring	summer	fall	white	yellow-orange	pink-red	lavender-purple	blue	green-brown	Flowers LAVENDER to PURPLE (Cont.)		woods	dry woods	wet woods	dunes	meadows	swamps	bogs	swales	aquatic	shores
D		●	●	●			●			Mint, Wild	98					●					
C		●	●	●		●	●	●		Monkey Flower, Square-stemmed	96						●	●	●		
D		●		●			●			Motherwort	98	●							●		
C		●	●				●	●		Nightshade	96						●		●		
C		●	●	●		●	●	●		Orchid, Purple Fringed	98					●	●		●		
C		●	●			●	●			Peppermint	98					●			●		
B	●	●					●	●		Phlox, Wood	90	●									
C	●	●	●	●		●	●	●		Self-heal	92					●					
C		●	●			●	●			Spearmint	98					●			●		
B		●					●			Thistle, Marsh	96					●			●		
B	●	●					●	●		Vetch, Hairy	90					●					
C	●						●	●		Violet, Bird-foot	90		●								
C		●		●			●			Waterleaf, Virginia	92	●							●		
										Flowers BLUE											
D	●			●			●	●		Blue-eyed Grass	100					●					
C	●			●				●		Blue-eyed Mary	98	●							●		
B		●	●	●		●	●	●		Blueweed	102					●					
B		●	●	●		●	●	●		Chicory	104					●					
C	●	●	●	●	●		●			Forget-me-not	102	●				●	●		●		
C		●	●	●			●	●		Gentian, Closed	104	●				●			●		●
C		●	●	●			●	●		Gentian, Fringed	104	●				●			●		●
C	●	●		●		●		●		Harebell	102		●		●	●					
B	●	●						●		Iris, Blue	100						●		●		
C	●			●			●	●		Iris, Dwarf Lake	100							●			●
C		●	●					●		Lobelia, Great	104					●	●		●		●
B	●	●		●		●	●	●		Lupine	100					●					
B		●		●		●	●	●		Lupine, Garden	100					●					
C	●	●						●		Periwinkle	102	●				●					
C		●	●					●		Pickerelweed	102									●	
D		●	●	●		●	●	●		Skullcap, Common	104					●	●				●
D	●	●	●	●			●	●		Speedwell, Common	102	●		●		●					
B		●	●				●	●		Vervain, Blue	104					●	●		●		
C	●						●	●		Violet, Common Blue	100	●				●					
										Flowers GREEN and BROWN											
D	●								●	Arrow-grass, Seaside	106						●	●			●
B	●	●							●	Cat-tail, Common	106						●	●	●	●	

visibility rating	season of bloom			flower color						Guide (cont.) Flowers GREEN and BROWN	page	habitats									
	spring	summer	fall	white	yellow-orange	pink-red	lavender-purple	blue	green-brown			woods	dry woods	wet woods	dunes	meadows	swamps	bogs	swales	aquatic	shores
C	•	•							•	Cat-tail, Narrow-leaved	106						•	•	•	•	
D		•	•			•			•	Dock, Curled	106					•					
C		•					•		•	Gentian, Spurred	106			•			•	•			
C		•				•			•	Ground Nut	106									•	•
D		•					•		•	Helleborine	108	•									
D		•							•	Orchid, Tall Northern Bog	108			•			•	•	•		
C		•	•						•	Ragweed	108				•	•					
D	•				•	•			•	Skunk Cabbage	106						•		•		
C	•	•				•	•		•	Spurge, Cypress	108					•					
D		•					•		•	Twayblade, Heartleaf	108			•			•	•			
C		•	•	•					•	Wormwood, Tall	108					•					

Glossary

annual – living for a single growing season

axil – the angle between a leaf or branch and the main axis

bicolored – of two colors

bract – a small, rudimentary or imperfectly developed leaf

calyx – sepals collectively form the calyx

corolla – all the petals of a flower make the corolla

chlorophyll – the green pigment in plants that permits the conversion of light energy to food through photosynthesis

cleft – a deep lobe or cut usually applied to leaf margins

entire – without teeth, serrations, or lobes, as leaf margins

exudate – material that has oozed to the surface, usually of a stem or leaf

head – a dense collection of sessile or nearly sessile flowers as in the Composite family

hybridize – the process by which two plants that differ in one or more basic characteristics produce offspring

lateral – on or arising from the side

linear – a long and narrow organ (leaf) with the sides nearly parallel

midrib – middle vein in a leaf

node – the part of a stem where the leaf, leaves, or secondary branches emerge

"petal" – when the word petal occurs in quotation marks it is not a true petal.

prostrate – extended in a horizontal position; trailing on the ground

recurved – curved backward or downward

rhizome – an elongated underground stem

sac – a pouch within a plant often containing fluid

sepal – one member of the calyx

sessile – refers to a flower or leaf lacking a stalk

stipule – a small, leaf-like appendage at the base of a leafstalk in some plants. Usually found in pairs.

toxic – poisonous

tuber – a modified branch, usually underground and for storage of food

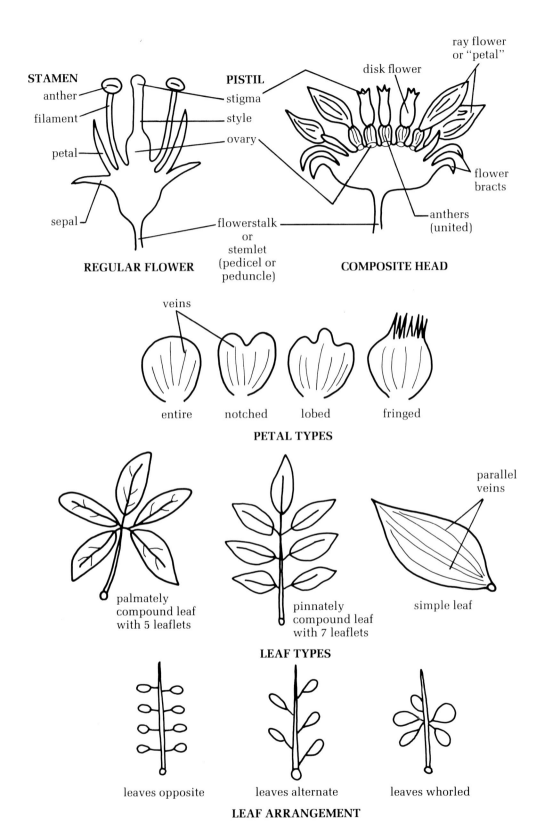

STAMEN
anther
filament
petal
sepal

PISTIL
stigma
style
ovary

flowerstalk
or
stemlet
(pedicel or
peduncle)

REGULAR FLOWER

ray flower
or "petal"
disk flower

flower
bracts

anthers
(united)

COMPOSITE HEAD

veins

entire   notched   lobed   fringed

PETAL TYPES

palmately
compound leaf
with 5 leaflets

pinnately
compound leaf
with 7 leaflets

parallel
veins

simple leaf

LEAF TYPES

leaves opposite   leaves alternate   leaves whorled

LEAF ARRANGEMENT

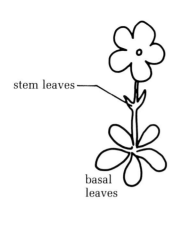

stem leaves

basal leaves

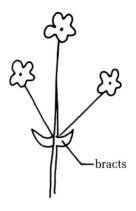

bracts

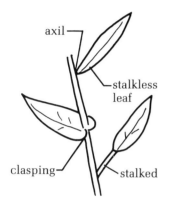

axil

stalkless leaf

clasping

stalked

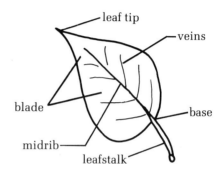

leaf tip

veins

blade

base

midrib

leafstalk

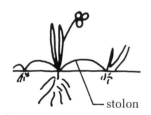

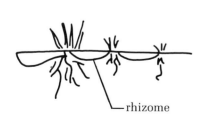

stolon

rhizome

stipules

tendril

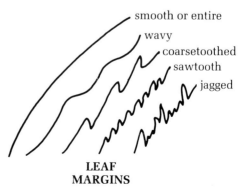

smooth or entire

wavy

coarsetoothed

sawtooth

jagged

LEAF MARGINS

White Flowers

Flowers placed in this section are those ranging from pure white through cream, greenish-white, yellowish-white, and pearly-white.

Also included are those flowers that are basically white but have various colored spots, lines, streaks, or tints.

Pages 24-53

Although found in groups (colonies) Canada anemone seldom covers extensive areas and, therefore, is assigned a "B" Visibility Rating.

Yellow and Orange Flowers

Flowers in this section are yellow and orange and include those that are described as greenish-yellow, orange-yellow, yellow-orange, and red-orange.

Pages 54-71

A mixture of Smoothish Hawkweed, Orange Hawkweed, and Ox-eye Daisy in a meadow habitat along an Upper Peninsula highway. These species all have an "A" Visibility Rating.

Pink to Red Flowers

Includes flowers that are definitely pink to red and also the variations of dusky pink, crimson, and rose. Also some bi-colored flowers containing pink with some other color are in this group.

Pages 72-89

The color groupings of "PINK and RED" flowers, "LAVENDER and PURPLE" flowers, and "BLUE" flowers may be more of a hindrance than a help. Few people would agree on many of the hues, tints, and shades encountered in these colors. So please be patient and if you don't find the flower that to you is certainly pink, for example, try the other color categories.

Cardinal flower, a plant of striking beauty from late summer into fall, is given a "B" Visibility Rating because it rarely forms extensive masses of color.

Lavender to Purple Flowers

Includes flowers that are some shade of purple, ranging from lavender to violet, magenta, red-purple, and dark purple.

Pages 90-99

Purple loosestrife is often found in extensive patches which, along with its bright color ranging from purple to pink, is given an "A" Visibility Rating. A plant of swales, marshy lake beaches, river banks, and other moist areas.

Blue Flowers

Flowers that are unquestionably blue are placed here, but there are some of borderline shades, such as violet-blue.

Pages 98-105

Garden Lupine is an escape from the gardens of the early settlers and patches of these showy flowers are now found growing wild, particularly in the western Upper Peninsula.

Green and Brown Flowers

Although the flowers in this group are basically green, some of them have parts marked with brown or purple or brownish-purple.

Pages 106-109

Because of their flower color, plants such as Tall wormwood and the others in this group require close attention to determine that the flowers are present as they may be casually mistaken for seeds or leaves.

BROADLEAF TOOTHWORT
or Pepperwort
Dentaria diphylla Michx.
Mustard family   Cruciferae

woods   spring   8-12 in. (20-30 cm)

Blossoms are formed at tip of stem in a loose, open cluster of 4-petaled flowers. Color is white changing to pink as the blossoms mature.

A single pair of leaves on the stem, somewhat above the center of the plant, nearly opposite each other, and each divided into 3 broad leaflets which are up to 1 in. (2.5 cm) across and coarsely toothed.

Stem is smooth and unbranched. Colonies of plants are common.

CUTLEAF TOOTHWORT
Dentaria laciniata Muhl.
Mustard family   Cruciferae

woods   spring   8-12 in. (20-30 cm)

Also has 4-petaled white flowers and is similar to *D. diphylla* but has 3 stem leaves, each divided into 3 long, narrow, deeply cleft, sharp pointed leaflets.

Stem is hairy on the upper part.

SPRING CRESS
Cardamine bulbosa Schreb.
Mustard family   Cruciferae

woods, swales   spring   8-25 in. (2-6 dm)

A cluster of 4-petaled white flowers that may be pink tinted are at the tip of the stem. Stem leaves are alternate, stalkless, margins entire or with a few very coarse teeth or lobes. Basal leaves are long-stalked, round or kidney-shaped.

Stems may be either smooth or fuzzy.

Fruits are erect, narrow, elongated pods with pointed tips.

MITREWORT or Bishop's cap
Mitella diphylla L.
Saxifrage family   Saxifragaceae

woods   spring   8-18 in. (2-5 dm)

Flowers are small, white, cup-shaped with lacy fringes. There are 5-20 flowers borne singly along the upper 2-6 in. (5-15 cm) of the stem.

Most of the leaves arise from the base of the plant on long stalks. There is also a pair of stalkless, 3-lobed leaves opposite each other about midway on the stem.

Stems are mostly fuzzy especially below the stem leaves.

NAKED MITREWORT
Mitella nuda L.
Saxifrage family   Saxifragaceae

swamps, bogs   spring, summer
2-8 in. (5-20 cm)

Similar to M. diphylla but can be distinguished by the following:

1. the entire plant is smaller
2. the flowers are more yellow-green than white
3. the fringes on the petals are more thread-like
4. the stem leaves are lacking or there may be 1 leaf present but not 2
5. the basal leaves are smaller, rounder, and indented at the base
6. the flowers are borne on the upper 1-4 in. (2-10 cm) of the stem
7. it is usually found in wetter habitats
8. and it blooms a little later in the season.

GOLDTHREAD
Coptis trifolia (L.) Salisb.
Crowfoot family   Ranunculaceae

bogs, swamps, wet woods   spring
3-6 in. (8-15 cm)

Delicate white flowers on long flowerstalks arising from the base of plant. Sepals appear as petals, 5-7 in number. Petals are club-shaped and inconspicuous. There are many stamens. There is but one flower on each very fine flowerstalk and it usually projects above the leaves.

The palmately compound leaves arise from the base of the plant, leaflets 3 in number, smooth, shiny on upper surface, dark-green, margins round-toothed; remain green all winter.

Broadleaf
Toothwort

C

Mitrewort   C

Cutleaf
Toothwort

C

Naked
Mitrewort

C

Spring
Cress

C

Goldthread   D

FOAMFLOWER or False Mitrewort
Tiarella cordifolia L.
Saxifrage family   Saxifragaceae

woods   spring   6-12 in. (15-30 cm)

Delicate white flowers on short stemlets from a somewhat fuzzy central stem. The long, slender, rod-like stamens arise between the petals.

Leaves are only at the base of the plant on long, definitely fuzzy leafstalks. Blade (wide part) of the leaf is broad, 3-5 lobed, and is indented at the base.

PLEASE DO NOT PICK

STARFLOWER
Trientalis borealis Raf.
Primrose family   Primulaceae

bogs, swamps, woods   late spring, early summer   4-10 in. (1-2.5 dm)

Flowers white with 5-9 but usually 7 sharp pointed petals. Commonly a pair of flowers at the tip of the plant but may vary from 1-4. Flowerstalk thin and wiry. Stamens prominent and same number as petals.

The shiny, long tapered leaves form a single whorl below the flower, 5-10 in number, 2-4 in. (4-10 cm) long,; margins mostly smooth. There may be a leaf below the whorl but, if present, is very small.

PLEASE DO NOT PICK

DUTCHMAN'S BREECHES
Dicentra Cucullaria (L.) Berhn.
Fumitory family   Fumariaceae

woods   spring   6-12 in. (15-30 cm)

White, waxy, inflated flowers dangle from the stem like tiny pantaloons. There are 2 spurs spreading and extending backward (upward) forming the legs of the breeches. Flowers are yellow-tipped.

Leaves are very finely divided, delicate, long-stalked, and arise from the base of the plant.

WILD LILY-OF-THE-VALLEY or Canada Mayflower
Maianthemum canadense Desf.
Lily family   Liliaceae

woods   spring   2-8 in. (5-20 cm)

Small, individual white flowers clustered together at the tip of the stem to form a delicate, sweet-smelling flower head. Each flower is 4-part (2 petals and 2 petal-like sepals) and each has 4 rod-like projecting stamens.

Leaves usually 2 per plant but may be 1 or 3, the heart-shaped base partially surrounds the stem; leaf veins are parallel, each one extending from the base to the tip of the leaf.

Fruit is a cluster of green berries with reddish speckles, turning light red as it matures. Not edible.

BLOODROOT
Sanguinaria canadensis L.
Poppy family   Papaveraceae

moist woods   spring   2-6 in. (5-15 cm)

A single flower that has white petals and yellow rod-like filaments at its center. Petals usually 8 but sometimes 10 and (rarely) as many as 16. Often 4 petals are longer than the others imparting a square appearance to the blossom. Flowers close in cold or cloudy weather.

Leaves arise from the base of the plant, are rounded in general outline; margin is wavy to coarsely toothed. Blade is up to 4″ (10 cm) across at flowering time, growing larger, up to 10″ (26 cm) after flowers fade.

Stems are smooth, erect, leafless, and contain a red juice that can cause a rash or blistering of the skin.

PLEASE DO NOT PICK

SQUIRREL CORN
Dicentra canadensis (Goldie) Walp.
Fumitory family   Fumariaceae

woods   spring   6-12 in. (15-30 cm)

Similar to D. Cucullaria but flowers are more heart-shaped with rounded spurs. It tends to be a little later in blooming so that Squirrel corn may be at its prime when Dutchman's Breeches are fading.

The two are often found growing side by side.

Foamflower

C

Wild lily-of-the-valley   C

Bloodroot

C

Starflower   C

Dutchman's
Breeches

C

Squirrel
Corn

C

WOOD ANEMONE
Anemone quinquefolia L.
Crowfoot family   Ranunculaceae

woods   spring   4-8 in. (1-2 dm)

A single flower up to 1 in. (2.5 cm) across at tip of stem; white (may be pinkish on lower surface), without petals but the sepals appear as petals, usually 5-6 in number. A central tuft of white to yellowish stamens is quite noticeable.

Compound leaves are in a whorl, usually 3, midway on stem. Each leaf is composed of 3-5 deeply cleft and coarsely toothed leaflets. There may be a long-stalked leaf from the base of the plant that is similar in form to the stem leaves.

Usually found in colonies.

CANADA ANEMONE
Anemone canadensis L.
Crowfoot family   Ranunculaceae

meadows, swales   spring, early summer   1-2 ft. (3-6 dm)

A single flower born at the tip of the stem; "petals" white (actually are sepals) are 5 in. number. Flowers 1-1½ in. (2.5-4 cm) across.

Stem leaves are large, stalkless, deeply cleft, coarsely toothed, sharp pointed, in whorls of 2-3 midway up stem. Basal leaves are similar but long-stalked.

Seed head is round, ball-like, covered with spines that have curved, pointed tips.

Usually found in colonies.

WATER ARUM or Wild Calla
Calla palustris L.
Arum family   Araceae

swamps, bogs, ponds   spring
6-16 in. (1.5-4 dm)

"Flower" is a showy, white, oval and sharp pointed bract whose base embraces the stem. Within this structure and terminating the stem is the green, fleshy and knobby spike bearing tiny, white flowers. "Flowerstalk" is long, leafless, and arises from base of plant which is usually submerged in the water.

Heart-shaped, smooth and shiny leaves with stalks that are about equal to the length of the blades arise from the base of the plant.

TRAILING ARBUTUS
Epigaea repens L.
Heath family   Ericaceae

dry woods   spring   prostrate

Flowers are 5-petaled, white to pale pink, fragrant, formed in clusters, and are usually hidden beneath the dead leaves on the forest floor.

Leaves are oval-shaped, thick and leathery; margins entire.

PROTECTED MICHIGAN WILD FLOWER   DO NOT DISTURB

BUNCHBERRY or Dwarf Cornel
Cornus canadensis L.
Dogwood family   Cornaceae

swamps, woods   late spring, summer   8-10 in. (20-26 cm)

What appears to be the flower are 4 white, showy "petals" (actually modified leaves) surrounding the cluster of greenish to cream-colored true flowers in the center.

Leaves are dull green above and shiny below, have prominent and parallel veins, are rounded with pointed tips, and form a whorl or circle of 6 near the top of the plant.

Stems are ridged and woody.

Fruit is a cluster of shiny, red berries; not toxic but bland. Usually found in colonies.

BIRDSEYE PRIMROSE
Primula mistassinica Michx.
Primrose family   Primulaceae

rocks, shores spring 4-10 in. (10-25 cm)

Flowers mostly white with a faint pink or lavender tint but occasionally lavender colored flowers are found. The 5 petals each have a notched tip. At the center of the flower is a noticeable yellow circle or "eye". Stamens and pistil are hidden in the tube below the petals.

Leaves are ¾-2 ¾ in. (2-7 cm) long, are oval and tapering to the base, found only as a basal rosette. Margins are smooth to slightly toothed.

Wood
Anemone

C

Trailing Arbutus   D

Canada
Anemone

B

Bunchberry   C

Water
Arum

C

Birdseye Primrose   D

TRILLIUM or Large-flowered Trillium
Trillium grandiflorum (Michx.) Salisb.
Lily family   Liliaceae

woods   spring   12-18 in. (3-5 dm)

Large, white, 3-petaled flowers, 2-3 in.
(5-7.5 cm) across, a single flower per
stem; 3 prominent, pointed, green sepals
occur below and between the somewhat
longer petals.

3 leaves emerge from a single point on
the stem (whorl); leaves broad, rapidly
narrowing to a pointed tip; leaf veins
conspicuous; one set of leaves per plant.

The white flowers turn pink with age.
Also, a disease caused by a mycoplasma-
like organism results in varying degrees
of green discoloration of the petals ranging from a narrow green streak to a completely green blossom.

PROTECTED MICHIGAN WILDFLOWER   DO NOT DISTURB

MAY APPLE or Mandrake
Podophyllum peltatum L.
Barberry family   Berberidaceae

open woods spring 12-18 in. (30-46 cm)

Flowers white, fragrant, nodding on
short, stout, fuzzy stalks that arise from
the fork of the two leaves; one flower
per plant. Stamens yellow, rod-like,
surround the pistil. The inflated pistil is
yellow to yellow-green.

Flowering plants have two deeply
lobed leaves that overtop the nodding
blossom. Immature plants have one
umbrella-like leaf.

Fruit is large, lemon shape, edible, not
tasty. Plants grow in colonies. Seeds,
leaves, and roots are toxic.

RUE ANEMONE
Anemonella thalictroides (L). Spach.
Crowfoot family   Ranunculaceae

woods   spring   4-10 in. (1-2.5 dm.)

5-10 petal-like white to pale pink sepals
that resemble petals. Flowers about ¾
in. across (2 cm.) with 2 or more of them
in a loose cluster beneath which is a
whorl of blunt-lobed leaflets. Basal
leaves long-stalked each with three
groups of 3 leaflets, rounded at their
base and bluntly lobed at their tips.

FALSE RUE ANEMONE, Isopyrum biter-
natum (Raf.) T.&G. (not shown) is similar
in appearance but has smaller flowers
(½ in.) and leaflets much more deeply
lobed at their tips. Flowers usually

single. Both species found in southern
part of the Lower Peninsula.

NODDING TRILLIUM
Trillium cernuum L.
Lily family   Liliaceae

woods   spring, early summer
6-20 in. (1.5-5 dm)

Similar to T. *grandiflorum*, the most
apparent differences being the 3-petaled
flower dangles below the leaves on a
gently curving flowerstalk and the anthers are pink rather than pale yellow.

PROTECTED MICHIGAN WILDFLOWER   DO NOT DISTURB

SWEET CICELY
Osmorhiza Claytoni (Michx.) Clarke
Parsley family   Umbelliferae

woods late spring 18-36 in. (4.5-9 dm)

Sparse, often scraggly clusters of white
to greenish-white flowers that are quite
inconspicuous. The small blossoms
radiate from a central point like a
bursting rocket.

Leaves are pinnately compound with
each one divided into 3-5 segments;
often each segment is again divided into
3 leaflets. Leaf margins are decidedly
coarsely toothed. There are often 1 or 2
basal leaves that are similar to the stem
leaves. Appearance of leaves may be
fern-like, especially in newer, smaller
upper leaves. Stems are upright and
have some degree of hairiness varying
from slight to dense.

CANADA VIOLET
Viola canadensis L.
Violet family   Violaceae

woods   spring, early summer
6-16 in. (1.5-4 dm)

Flowers with 5 white petals, the lower 3
marked at their base with conspicuous,
fine, brown-purple veins. Back side of
petals is tinged blue or purple. Center of
flower is yellow. Flowers and leaves are
on the same stem.

Leaves are found both on the stem and
at the base of the plant; basal leaves
with very long stalks, roughly 3 times
the length of the blades. Stem leafstalks
are shorter; blades heart-shaped with
sawtooth margins.

Stems are smooth to somewhat downy.

One of at least 21 species of violets in
the area.

Trillium   B   Nodding Trillium   D

May
Apple

C

Sweet
Cicely

D

Rue
Anemone

C

Canada
Violet

C

31

DWARF GINSENG
Panax trifolium L.

Ginseng family   Araliaceae

woods, clearings   spring
4-8 in. (10-20 cm)

A rounded cluster of small, white flowers at the tip of the plant; 5 petals and 5 stamens; stamens protrude beyond the petals; flower-stalk arises from a whorl of leaves.

Whorl of leaves is near top of stem, usually 3 in number, palmately compound, each with 3-7 stalkless leaflets; margins finely toothed. Fruit is a yellow berry. Toxicity unknown. Not the ginseng of commerce.

SARSAPARILLA
Aralia nudicaulis L.

Ginseng family   Araliaceae

woods   late spring   8-20 in.   (2-5 dm)

Commonly 3 (but sometimes 4) balls of tiny white to greenish flowers from a single, leafless stalk that appears to come from the ground. Each flower has 5 petals that may be tinged with green or purple. Flowers occur beneath the leaves.

There is only one leaf but appears to be 3. The main leafstalk starts at ground level and terminates in 3 divisions; each subdivision of this compound leaf has 5 leaflets that are egg-shaped with long pointed tips and sawtooth margins.

Fruit is a blue-black berry; not edible.

BRISTLY SARSAPARILLA, *Aralia hispida* Vent. (not shown) is related but flower clusters on same stem as the leaves and above them. Lower stem is very bristly. Plants are larger (up to 3 ft. or 1 m. tall), bloom later (midsummer), usually on sandier, more open sites. Fruit is also a black berry, inedible.

FLOWERING SPURGE
Euphorbia corolatta L.

Spurge family   Euphorbiaceae

dry woods, meadows   summer-fall
1-3½ ft. (3-10 dm)

White flowers in open clusters radiating from a whorl of leaves. 5 rounded white bracts resembling petals surround a small cluster of tiny true flowers.

Leaves are long, narrow, stalkless, with smooth margins. Form whorls in upper part of plant, but alternate, single leaves below.

Stems upright and contain milky juice.

CATNIP or Catmint
Nepeta Cataria L.

Mint family   Labiatae

meadows   spring to fall   1-4 ft. (3-12 dm)

Individual flowers are tiny, borne in tight clusters at tips of stems. Petals are white with pink or purple spots.

Leaves are arrowhead-shaped with jagged tooth margins, are opposite each other in pairs, 1-3 in. (2.5-8 cm) long, and a lighter color on the underside.

Stems are 4-sided, erect, and covered with fine fuzzy hairs.

PITCHER'S THISTLE
Cirsium Pitcheri (Torr.) T. & G.

Composite family   Compositae

dune sand   spring to fall
up to 3 ft. (9 dm)

Flowers are creamy white to pale yellow. There are prickle-tipped, modified leaves (bracts) on the lower part of the flower head.

Leaves are stalkless, deeply cleft into narrow lobes that are either smooth at the tips or end in a small, weak spine.

Stem and lower leaf surfaces are densely white-woolly.

Stems are erect and lack spines except in area where leaves attach to the stem.

A THREATENED SPECIES
DO NOT DISTURB

LYRE-LEAVED ROCK CRESS
Arabis lyrata L.

Mustard family   Cruciferae

dunes, rocks   spring to fall
up to 14 in. (3.5 dm)

Flowers are about ¼ in. (5 mm) across with 4 rounded, white petals.

Leaves on the stem are few and scattered, long, narrow, and tapered to the base; margins are usually entire but there may be a few slightly toothed leaves on the lower stem. At the base of the plant is a rosette of narrow but deeply lobed leaves.

Stems are upright or somewhat reclining, smooth in upper portion and sometimes fuzzy near the base.

Fruit is a long, narrow pod up to 1½ in. (4 cm) long and only about ¹⁄₁₆ in. (1-2 mm) wide. Pods tend to point upward.

white

Catnip

C

Dwarf Ginseng   D

Sarsaparilla

D

Pitcher's
Thistle

D

Flowering
Spurge

B

Lyre-leaved
Rock Cress

C

BUCKBEAN
Menyanthes trifoliata L.
Gentian family   Gentianaceae

bogs, ponds, swamps   spring, early summer   4-12 in. (1-3 dm)

Flowers are white, sometimes tinged with pink, tubular at the base and flaring to 5 recurved lobes which are conspicuously fringed on the inner surface.

Leaves are palmately compound with 3 shiny leaflets on a long stalk arising from the base of the plant. Leaflets are 1-3 in. (2.5-7 cm) long.

Plants are usually found in shallow water.

**PROTECTED MICHIGAN WILDFLOWER
DO NOT DISTURB**

BEARBERRY or Kinnikinick
Arctostaphylos Uva-ursi (L.) Spreng.
Heath family   Ericaceae

dunes, rocky areas   spring, early summer   up to 12 in. (3 dm)

Flowers are white, white tinged with pink, or pink. Oval in shape, constricted at the mouth then flaring into 5 spreading lobes. Flowers in clusters of 5-10 at end of branches.

Leaves smooth, leathery, shiny on upper side, persistent year-round, rounded at terminal ends but tapering at the base; margins entire.

Stems mostly prostrate with branches upright, woody with red to gray bark, creeping.

Fruit is a bright red, edible berry. Dry.

CLUSTERED BROOM-RAPE
Orobanche fasciculata Nutt.
Broom-rape family   Orobanchaceae

dune sand   spring, summer
2-6 in. (5-15 cm)

Flowers usually white but may be yellow or purple, up to 1 in. (2.5 cm) long, with 5 nearly equal lobes. Calyx is downy, tubular with flaring lobes.

Leaves are white, scale-like.

Stems reddish. Plants parasitic, usually on wormwood in this area. As with parasitic plants chlorophyll is absent, thus no green coloration.

**A THREATENED SPECIES
DO NOT DISTURB**

GREENBRIER
Smilax hispida Muhl.
Lily family   Liliaceae

swales   spring, early summer   vine

Ragged, open clusters of greenish-white to green flowers, each cluster arising in a leaf axil. Flowerstalk is at least twice as long as the adjacent leafstalk.

Leaves are thin, comparatively large (3-5 in. or 8-12 cm long). Somewhat roundish but with pointed tips. Threadlike tendrils arise from the leaf axils.

Greenish prickles are found along the stem. These turn dark with age. Prickles often few and scattered on upper stem becoming dense to extremely dense on the lower part.

Fruit is a cluster of dark blue to black, inedible berries.

LESSER STITCHWORT
Stellaria graminea L.
Pink family   Caryophyllaceae

woods, clearings   spring to mid-summer   12-20 in. (3-5 dm)

The white flowers are borne on spreading flowerstalks. The flowers appear to have 10 petals but actually there are only 5 that are deeply notched to about one half the length of the petal.

Leaves in pairs and opposite, ½-2 in. (1.5-5 cm) long, narrow, margins smooth.

STARWORT
Stellaria longipes Goldie
not shown

Has similar flowers but they are borne on erect stalks and the petals are more deeply cleft. Plants are shorter. Supposedly limited to the Grand Sable Dunes area in Michigan..

ENCHANTER'S NIGHTSHADE
Circaea quadrisulcata (Maxim.)
Evening primrose family   Onagraceae

woods   summer   1-2 ft. (3-6 dm.)

Flowers small, white, sparsely scattered on upright, multiple flowerstalks from a single stem. The 2 petals are so deeply notched as to appear as 4. There are 2 recurved sepals.

Leaves are simple, egg-shaped with pointed tips, opposite on long leafstalks; toothed. Fruit is a small bur covered with hooked bristles.

white

Buckbean

D

Greenbrier   D

Lesser
Stitchwort

D

Bearberry   C

Clustered Broom-rape   D

Enchanter's Nightshade   C

35

WILD STRAWBERRY
Fragaria virginiana Duchesne.
Rose family   Rosaceae

meadows, open woods   late spring,
early summer   3-6 in. (8-15 cm)

White flowers are ½-1 in. (1.2-2.5 cm)
across with 5 rounded petals, numerous
yellow stamens. Flowers and leaves are
on separate stalks, both arising from
near the ground line and flowerstalks
usually shorter than the leafstalks.

Leaves are compound with 3 blunt-
toothed leaflets; leafstalks and underside
of leaflets finely hairy.

Fruit is a red berry, fragrant, and bearing
seeds in sunken pits on the surface;
edible and delicious. The related
WOODLAND STRAWBERRY, Frageria
vesca L. (not shown) has fruits that bear
seeds on the surface, not in pits, the
plants are usually smaller, flowers are
smaller and borne on stalks usually
longer than the leafstalks. Both species
are low plants spreading by runners.

THREE-TOOTHED CINQUEFOIL
Potentilla tridentata Soland.
Rose family   Rosaceae

dry sand, rock crevices   spring,
summer   4-12 in. (1-3 dm)

Spreading clusters of 5-petaled white
flowers with the flowerstalks rising above
a mat of leaves. Numerous stamens are
white with pinkish anthers.

Leaves palmately compound with 3 leaflets, each somewhat wedge-shaped. The
side margins of the leaflets are entire
and hairy but the tip terminates in 3
rounded but sharply pointed teeth. Upper
leaf surface is bright green turning brilliant red; lower surface covered with tan-
nish fuzz; leafstalks have long white hairs.

STICKY FALSE ASPHODEL
Tofieldia glutinosa (Michx)
Lily family   Liliaceae

Wet or moist areas   summer
20 in. (5 dm)

The cluster of white flowers at the tip of
the stem have short flowerstalks. Petals
6 and stamens 6 with pink anthers. There
are a few long and narrow leaves that
sheath the stem near the base of the plant.

Stem (and flowerstalks) covered with
short, sticky, black hairs. Fruits are red,
globular capsules.

BLADDER CAMPION
Silene Cucubalus Wibel.
Pink family   Caryophyllaceae

meadows spring, summer 8-30 in. (2-8 dm)

Open clusters of 5-30 white flowers
each with 5 deeply notched petals arising from a greatly inflated, smooth, 5-
lobed, bell-shaped sac (calyx) which is
about ½ in. (13 mm) long, has a papery
texture, usually pinkish, and often has
many, netted green or red-colored veins.
The thread-like styles project well
beyond the petals.

Leaves are in pairs, 1-3 in. (3-8 cm) long,
much longer than broad; margins are
entire. Leaves are stalkless often clasping
the stem and are smooth.

Stems are usually smooth but may be
hairy, and tend to recline on the ground
with age rather than remaining erect.

FLEABANE
Erigeron strigosus Muhl.
Composite family   Compositae

meadows spring to fall 2-4 ft. (6-12 dm)

Aster-like flowers, white to pale pink,
with 50-100 "petals" (ray flowers) which
are more numerous than on asters.

Leaves are narrow, mostly without teeth
on the margins but toothed leaves are
not too infrequent; basal leaves much
longer than broad, widest above the
center, up to 1 in. (2.5 cm) wide. Stem
leaves are much smaller, are long, narrow, and stalkless.

Stems are sparsely leafy, upright, slender, branching and rebranching near the
top. Stem and leaves are very hairy,
especially on the lower part of the plant.

BLACK SNAKEROOT
Sanicula marilandica L.
Parsley family   Umbelliferae

woods   spring, early summer
1-4 ft. (3-12 dm)

Flowers are white, sometimes described
as greenish-white or yellowish-white, or
green. Each blossom is a ball of tiny
flowers arising from a whorl of small
leaves below the blossom.

Basal leaves are palmately compound
each with 5 leaflets, the lower pair so
deeply cut as to appear as 7 leaflets;
margins are sawtooth to jagged.

Fruit is a bristly bur.

Wild Strawberry   C

Bladder Campion   A

Three-toothed
Cinquefoil

D

Fleabane   A

Sticky
False
Asphodel

C

Black
Snakeroot

D

DOGFENNEL or Stinking Chamomile
Anthemis Cotula L.
Composite family   Compositae

meadows   spring to fall
4-24 in. (1-6 dm)

Daisy-like flowers with 10-20 white "petals" that are ¼-⅓ in. (6-9 mm) long. Center is a domed, yellow disk. Flower is ¾-1 in. (1.9-2.5 cm) across.

Leaves are deeply cut and finely divided; ill smelling.

SCENTLESS CHAMOMILE
Matricaria maritima L.
not shown

Flowers similar to *Anthemis Cotula* but leaves are even more finely divided, odorless, and blossom later in the season (summer, early fall).

SMOOTH SOLOMON'S SEAL
Polygonatum biflorum (Walt.) Ell.
Lily family   Liliaceae

woods   late spring
18-24 in. (4.5-6 dm)

Tubular white to greenish-white flowers, ½-¾ in. (14-20 mm) long, usually dangling in pairs (may be 1-4) on slender flowerstalks from axils of leaves.

Leaves alternate, stalkless or even clasping, and have parallel veins which are not hairy; margins are smooth. Stem is unbranched and usually arched.

HAIRY SOLOMON'S SEAL
P. pubescens (Willd.) *Pursh.* (not shown)

Flowers are smaller than P. biflorum (less than ½ in.) and the leaf veins are minutely hairy on the lower surface.

PRAIRIE FALSE INDIGO or
White False Indigo
Baptisia leucantha T. & G.
Bean family   Fabaceae

meadows, woods   summer
3-6 ft. (1-2 m.)

Flowers mostly white but may have a tinge of purple; up to 1 in. long (2.5 cm) borne on an erect spike the flowering portion being up to 2 ft. long. Only one (or a few) flowering spikes per plant.

Leaves palmately compound, the 3 more or less roundish leaflets about 2 in. long (5 cm.). Drying leaves tend to turn black.

Fruit is a black 1-2 in. drooping pod.

FALSE SOLOMON'S SEAL
Smilacina racemosa (L.) Desf.
Lily family   Liliaceae

woods   spring, early summer
16-36 in. (4-9 dm)

Branched clusters of many, tiny, individual, creamy-white flowers borne at the tip of the stem.

Leaves are large and in a flat plane, a row each side of the stem, oval with pointed tips, 4-8 in. (10-20 cm) long and 1-3 in. (3-8 cm) wide; veins are prominent and parallel; leafstalks are very short. Stems are arched (neither standing upright nor reclining on the ground) and covered with fine hairs.

Fruit is a white berry spotted with brown, later turning red dotted with purple. Although the taste is not too bad the berry does have a very large seed. Not recommended for eating.

STARRY FALSE SOLOMON'S SEAL
Smilacina stellata (L.) Desf.
Lily family   Liliaceae

A plant similar to S. racemosa with these differences:
1. Flowers are fewer but larger, ¼-⅜ in. (6-9 mm) across
2. Leaves are narrower, longer, and lack leafstalks so that leaf blade clasps the stem
3. Fruits are green berries with black stripes or may be completely black. Berries may turn bronze color with age
4. More likely to be found in the open dunes than in or along wooded areas.

ROCK SANDWORT
Arenaria stricta Michx.
Pink family   Caryophyllaceae

dunes, rocks   early summer
6-9 in. (15-23 cm)

Flowers white, ½-¾ in. (12-20 mm) across, 5 petals each longer than broad.

Leaves needle-like, paired, often with clusters of smaller ones between the pair, leaves crowded into lower half of stem, upper half essentially without leaves.

Stems are wiry. Plants may form loose, mat-like colonies.

Dogfennel   C

False Solomon's Seal   C

Starry False
Solomon's
Seal

C

Smooth Solomon's Seal   D

Prairie False
Indigo

C

Rock Sandwort   C

BASTARD TOADFLAX
Comandra umbellata (L.) Nutt.
Sandalwood family   Santalaceae

dry woods, meadows, shores   spring, summer   up to 12 in. (3 dm)

Blossoms form a flat-topped cluster of white (may be green tinted), individually small, bell-shaped flowers with flaring tips resembling 5-pointed stars.

Leaves oblong-oval, ¾-1½ in. (2-4 cm) long, numerous and alternate, margins entire; veins obscure.

NORTHERN COMANDRA
Comandra livida Richards.
not shown

Is a smaller plant, prefers moister sites, and the fruit is a scarlet berry.

Comandras are parasitic with their roots attached to other woody plant roots.

MEADOWSWEET
Spirea alba DuRoi.
Rose family   Rosaceae

wet meadows, swales   summer up to 7 ft. (2 m)

A tapering spike of separated clusters of tiny flowers about ¼ in. (6 mm) across; petals usually white but may be slightly pink. Numerous projecting stamens give the flower head a fuzzy outline.

Leaves are 1¼-2½ in. (3-6 cm) long.

Margins are finely toothed; leaf surfaces essentially smooth. A woody-stem shrub.

MOTH MULLEIN
Verbascum Blattaria L.
Snapdragon family   Scrophulariaceae

meadows   summer-fall   1-3 ft. (3-9 dm.)

Flowers are white often tinged with purple or commonly, all yellow. Petals 5 in number; stamens have purplish beards and orange color anthers. Flowers in a terminal spike attached to plant stem by short flowerstalks that seldom exceed ⅝ in. (15 mm). Flowers 1 in. across (2.5 cm.).

Leaves are few and variable in shape and size, larger at bottom of plant; may have entire, toothed, or lobed margins. Leaves are smooth.

Stem upright, slender, fuzzy at top.

THIMBLEBERRY
Rubus parviflorus Nutt.
Rose family   Rosaceae

open woods, meadows   early summer   3-6 ft. (1-2 m)

Flowers white, showy, 1-2 in. (3-5 cm) across. Petals oval, 5 in number; stamens yellow and numerous; sepals 5, long pointed. Leaves large, 4-8 in. (10-20 cm) across, usually 5 lobes, margins coarsely and irregularly toothed, the veins are prominent.

Leaves resemble maple leaves in shape.

Fruit is a many seeded, thimble-shaped, red berry, edible but tart.

A shrub highly prized for its showy flowers and fruit that is excellent for jam.

WHITE BANEBERRY or Doll's-eyes
Actaea alba (L.) Mill.
Crowfoot family   Ranunculaceae

woods   early summer   1-3 ft. (3-9 dm)

Elongated, thimble-shaped, dense clusters of white flowers borne on thick flowerstalks; 4-10 petals and numerous stamens; sepals drop as the flower opens.

Leaves 2-3 times pinnately compound; leaflet surfaces smooth; margins sharply and irregularly toothed; lighter color on lower surface.

Fruit is a cluster of rather large, usually white berries each with a conspicuous dark spot (doll's eyes). Stalks bearing the ripe berries are red. Poisonous to eat.

RED BANEBERRY
Actaea rubra (Ait.) Willd.
Crowfoot family   Ranunculaceae

woods   early summer   1-3 ft. (3-9 dm)

Compared to *A. alba* the white flower cluster is usually more rounded than elongated, the flowerstalks (later becoming the fruitstalks) are finer and more delicate, and the dark spot on the berry is smaller and less conspicuous. Poisonous.

Note: There are white-berried "red" baneberries and red-berried "white" baneberries so fruit color can be misleading in identification.

Bastard Toadflax C

Thimbleberry B

Meadowsweet B

White Baneberry D

Moth Mullein C

Red Baneberry D

PURPLE MEADOW-RUE

Thalictrum dasycarpum Fisch. & Avé-Lall.
Crowfoot family   Ranunculaceae

swales, swamps, meadows   summer
3-7 ft. (1-2 m)

Sprays of dangling, white flowers the most conspicuous parts being the projecting, thread-like stamens. There are no petals and the sepals drop as they unfold. Flowers are usually well above the leaves at the top of the plant.

Leaves are 2-3 times compound, being divided, then divided again, and, finally, into 3 leaflets. Margins of leaflets may be entire but usually have 3 blunt lobes at their apex. Lower surface of leaflets is distinctly fuzzy.

Stems are thick, many, and usually purplish in color from which the species derives its common name.

EARLY MEADOW-RUE

Thalictrum dioicum L.
Crowfoot family   Ranunculaceae

woods, swales   early spring
12-28 in. (3-7 dm)

The many stamens at maturity are even more decidedly downward pointing than those of T. *dasycarpum*, are yellow to greenish-yellow, and the sepals green to purplish.

Leaves of both species are 2-3 times compound but T. *dioicum* leaflets are often inclined to have more than 3 lobes at the apex. Note that this plant blossoms much earlier in the season, is much smaller, and is more apt to be found in rich wooded areas. Also, it is more common in the southern part of the State than it is in the north.

PARTRIDGEBERRY

Mitchella repens L.
Madder family   Rubiaceae

dry woods   summer   prostrate

Flowers are in pairs, tubular and flaring into 4 (rarely 3, 5, or 6) white petals that are conspicuously hairy on their inner face. Pink blossoms occur but are very rare.

Leaves are in pairs, rounded, about ½ in. (12 mm) long, remain green all year.

Stems creeping, forming mats. Roots may be found along the stem.

Fruit is a red berry which persists through the winter. Edible but insipid.

Note: Since the berry rather than the flower is apt to attract attention this is the illustration used.

PEARLY EVERLASTING

Anaphalis margaritacea (L.) Benth. & Hook.
Composite family   Compositae

meadows   summer   up to 3 ft. (1 m)

Flower heads pearly-white with yellow centers, globular-shaped, densely packed, and borne on short stalks at top of stem.

Leaves densely white-woolly on underside, long-cottony above, alternate on stem, up to 5 in. (12 cm) long, and narrow.

Stems white-woolly. Plant dries well for winter bouquets.

WHITE SNAKEROOT

Eupatorium rugosum Houtt.
Composite family   Compositae

woods   summer, fall   1-5 ft. (3-15 dm)

Flat-topped clusters of tiny white flowers with 12-24 individual flowers in each cluster.

Leaves in pairs along the stem, egg-shaped with tip drawn out to a sharp point; margins sawtoothed. Leafstalks up to 1 in. (2.5 cm) long or longer on large leaves.

Stems smooth in upper portion, fuzzy to slightly hairy in lower.

OX-EYE DAISY or Marguerite

Chrysanthemum Leucanthemum
Composite family   Compositae

meadows   summer   1-3 ft. (3-9 dm)

Showy flowers with 15-30 white "petals" notched at tips, a yellow center disk depressed in its middle, each flower up to 2 in. (5 cm) across. "Petals" are wider than most asters or fleabanes.

Leaves are smooth or sparsely hairy. Stem leaves are stalkless, base of leaf often clasping the stem; length up to 2 in. (5 cm), narrow, dark green; margins coarsely toothed.

Stems are upright, smooth or sparsely hairy. Plants commonly found in extensive colonies.

white

Purple
Meadow-rue

B

Pearly
Everlasting

B

Early
Meadow-rue

D

White
Snakeroot

C

Partridgeberry   D

Ox-eye Daisy   A

COW PARSNIP
Heracleum lanatum Michx.
Parsley family   Umbelliferae

meadows   summer   up to 10 ft. (3 m)

Flat-topped clusters of white flowers form very large blossoms up to 8 in. (20 cm) across. Petals deeply notched at tip, those on outer edge of cluster larger than those on inside.

Leaves very large, commonly up to 12-18 in. (3-4.5 dm) across, compound with 3 coarsely toothed leaflets, hairy on under-side; leafstalks inflated and clasp stem.

Stem definitely ridged, woolly and hollow, up to 2 in. (5 cm) thick.

Plants are conspicuous because of their huge size.

WATER-HEMLOCK
Cicuta maculata L.
Parsley family   Umbelliferae

meadows, swamps, streambanks
summer, fall   3-6 ft. (1-2 m)

Starburst clusters of tiny, white flowers at tip of flowerstalks above the leaves. Clusters 2-4 in. (5-10 cm) across.

Leaves are 2 or 3 times pinnately compound (there are secondary leafstalks arising from the main leafstalk). Leaflets are long, narrow, sharp pointed, and have sawtooth margins.

Stem is smooth, coarse, erect, and many branched; often a tendency to have a purple color especially in lower portion.

All parts of this plant, and particularly the roots, are deadly poisonous when eaten.

WILD CARROT or Queen Anne's Lace
Daucus Carota L.
Parsley family   Umbelliferae

meadows   summer, fall   2-3 ft. (6-9 dm)

Flower head is a flat-topped cluster of small, creamy-white, individual flowers. There may be one or more dark colored flowers in the center. Immediately below the flower head are several 3-5 pronged, narrow, sharp pointed, modified leaves (bracts). Leaves are deeply and finely cut. The leafstalk is bristly. Stems are stiff, erect, and bristly. Plant has a strong carrot odor.

Caution: Handling the leaves may cause a skin rash in some people.

FIELD BINDWEED
Convolvulus arvensis L.
Morning Glory family
Convolvulaceae

dunes, meadows   summer   trailing

Flowers white, pink, or white tinged with pink. Petals are united into a funnel-shaped flower about 1 in. (2-3 cm) across.

Leaves opposite, minutely downy, the arrowhead-shaped blades attached to a short leafstalk.

Stems are prostrate, trailing, or twining on surrounding vegetation.

HOARY ALYSSUM
Berteroa incana (L.) DC.
Mustard family   Cruciferae

meadows   summer, early fall
1-2 ft. (3-6 dm)

Flowers white, tiny, in elongated clusters at tip of stem; the 4 petals are deeply notched,; sepals and flowerstalks are hairy. The stalkless leaves are much longer than broad, wider across the middle and tapering to both ends; margins are smooth.

Leaves and stems are covered with a pale hoary down

Stems are rigidly upright.

Seed pods are usually present below the flowers, are oval in shape but have pointed tips.

DUNE LILY or Death Camas
Zygadenus glaucus Nutt.
Lily family   Liliaceae

dunes, beaches summer 1-3 ft. (3-9 dm)

6 greenish-white "petals" that may also be bronze or purple on the underside. Each "petal" has a heart-shaped greenish gland at its base. These "petals" are actually 3 true petals and 3 sepals that look like petals.

Leaves are grass-like, found mostly at the base of the plant, are very long (up to 20 in. or 5 dm) and narrow, decreasing in size higher on the stem; leathery.

Stems are smooth and stiffly erect.

All parts of this plant are poisonous if eaten.

Cow
Parsnip

B

Field Bindweed   C

Water-
hemlock

C

Hoary Alyssum   C

Dune
Lily

D

Wild Carrot   A

45

GREEN SHINLEAF
Pyrola virens Schweigg.
Heath family   Ericaceae

dry woods   early summer
6-10 in. (1.5-2.5 dm)

Spikes of 2-13 white to greenish, waxy, green veined flowers with protruding styles.

Leaves all at base of plant, long-stalked, leaf blades shorter than leafstalks; blades rounded tapering to a point.

Stems mostly naked with, perhaps, one scale leaf about half way up.

SIDEBELLS or One-sided shinleaf
Pyrola secunda L.
Heath family   Ericaceae

woods, bogs   summer
4-10 in. (10-25 cm)

Flowers white to greenish arising from one side of flowerstalk.

Stalk often bent allowing blossoms to dangle as little bells.

Style is long and straight and exceeds the length of the petals.

Leaves basal, roundish, blades are longer than leafstalks.

SHINLEAF
Pyrola elliptica Nutt.
Heath family   Ericaceae

woods   summer   5-10 in. (13-26 cm)

White, nodding, waxy blossoms in a loose spike; 5 petals usually with green veins; a long, curving pistil extends beyond the petals.

Flowers are fragrant.

Leaves only at bottom of the plant with leaf blades longer than the leafstalks and longer than broad (up to 3 in. or 7 cm long).

Blade "flows" into leafstalk. Color is dull green.

Stem is smooth, leafless in upper portion.

Commonest of all the pyrolas.

PLEASE DO NOT PICK

WATER PARSNIP
Sium suave Walt.
Parsley family   Umbelliferae

swamps, meadows, swales   summer
up to 6 ft. (1.8 m.)

Blossoms are white, flat-topped clusters of tiny individual flowers at tips of flowerstalks which radiate from top of the stem or lateral branches.

Leaves alternate along the stem, are pinnately compound with 3-7 pairs of long, narrow leaflets whose margins are sharply toothed. Basal leaves are finely dissected.

Stem is strongly ridged branching mainly above its middle. Plant prefers wet areas.

WATER HEMLOCK (Page 44) has a smooth stem.

WOODNYMPH or One-Flowered Wintergreen
Moneses uniflora (L) Gray.
Heath family   Ericaceae

bogs, swales, swamps   summer
2-5 in. (5-13 cm)

A single white or pinkish flower nodding from tip of stem, ½-¾ in. (13-20 mm) across, and fragrant. Has a prominent, melon-like, green pistil with a protruding style; 5 waxy petals.

Leaves are at base of plant, small, short-stalked, round, shiny below, dull green above; margins may be smooth or finely toothed.

Note: Leaves seen at base of the plant in illustration are not those of Woodnymph.

WINTERGREEN or Checkerberry
Gaultheria procumbens L.
Heath family   Ericaceae

dry woods   summer
3-7 in. (8-18 cm)

Flowers are small, white, waxy, egg-shaped, nodding, single blossoms attached to a red-colored flowerstalk.

Leaves are thick, egg-shaped, shiny green, and occur at the top of the plant; persist year-round.

Stems are creeping, woody, and wiry.

Crushed leaves have the odor and taste of wintergreen.

Fruit is an edible red berry often persisting year-round.

white

Green
Shinleaf

D

Water
Parsnip

C

Sidebells

D

Woodnymph   D

Shinleaf

C

Wintergreen   D

47

INDIAN PIPE
Monotropa uniflora L.
Heath family   Ericaceae

woods, swamps   summer, early fall
5-10 in. (13-26 cm)

A single, nodding, tubular flower which is the same color as the stem; usually white but may be pinkish; entire plant turns black with age.

Leaves are rudimentary, scale-like, white to pink.

Stem is white to pink, smooth and waxy in appearance. A parasitic plant lacking chlorophyll thus no green coloration.

PLEASE DO NOT PICK

POISON IVY or Three-leaved ivy
Rhus radicans L.
Cashew family   Anacardiaceae

meadows, woods, dunes   early summer   prostrate or climbing vine

Very inconspicuous 5-petaled, small, white to greenish-white flowers, clustered in leaf axils.

Leaves have 3 leaflets from a common point, mostly oblong with a pointed tip, margins are entire but there may be one or more irregular lobes along the side; color is a shiny green turning to a brilliant red later in the season. Leaf size and shape are extremely variable.

Fruit is a cluster of white to grayish-white, shiny berries. The berries are poisonous. In fact, all parts of this plant are poisonous to touch, causing painful, itching blisters of the skin. Contact is to be avoided at any time of the year including the dormant season. Even smoke from burning plants carries the irritant and can cause the same symptoms as touching the plant.

Poison ivy may be erect as individual plants, may climb on fences, trees, or, most commonly, form mats over the surface of the ground.

A person is more apt to be attracted to the lustrous green or red leaves than to the flowers or fruit which are inconspicuous so remember the saying:
    LEAFLETS THREE, LET IT BE!

CULVER'S ROOT
Veronicastrum virginicum (L.) Farw.
Figwort family   Scrophulariaceae

meadows, open woods   summer
2-6 ft. (6-18 dm)

White or pink, tubular flowers in long tapering spikes; 2 stamens extend beyond the petals of each flower.

Long, narrow, pointed leaves in whorls of 3-6 around the stem; margins sawtoothed.

PALE PAINTED CUP
Castilleja septentrionalis Lindl.
Figwort family   Scrophulariaceae

sandy or gravelly shores, woods
summer   6-24 in. (1.5-6 dm)

What appear to be flowers are white to yellowish leafy bracts with the small, tubular white or yellowish flowers hidden among these. Leaves are long and narrow, 1-4 in. (3-10 cm) long, attached singly and alternately along the stem; margins are smooth.

Stems are upright, ridged, and sometimes streaked.

See Indian paintbrush, *Castilleja coccinea*.

**A THREATENED SPECIES
DO NOT DISTURB**

COW WHEAT
Melampyrum lineare Desr.
Figwort family   Scrophulariaceae

woods, bogs, rock crevices   summer
4-12 in. (1-3 dm)

Tubular, white flowers with a yellow tip on the lower lip, found in leaf axils (where leaf joins the stem).

Leaves in pairs, long and narrow, margins usually smooth except upper leaves may be toothed near their base.

Stems are purplish and fuzzy.

TURTLEHEAD
Chelone glabra L.
Figwort family   Scrophulariaceae

swales, wet meadows   summer, fall
18-36 in. (4.5-9 dm)

Flowers are tubular, creamy-white, sometimes tinged with pink or purple, formed in tight, upright clusters at tip of the stem.

Leaves are in pairs along the stem, are stalkless, long, narrow, and sawtooth along the margins.

white

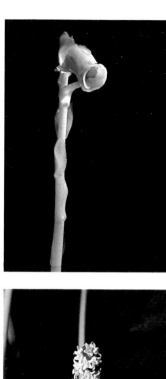

Indian Pipe

D

Pale
Painted Cup

C

Poison Ivy

D

Cow
Wheat

D

Culver's
Root

B

Turtlehead

B

49

ROUND-LEAVED SUNDEW
Drosera rotundifolia L.
Sundew family   Droseraceae

bogs, swamps   summer
up to 9 in. (23 cm)

Flowers (not present) are white to pink, tiny, 1/16-1/4 in. (4-7 mm) across; 3-15 in a loose spike on a tall flowerstalk.

The leaves are the conspicuous part of the plant being basal, with round, saucer-shaped blades on long, flattened leafstalks, the entire leaf covered with bristly red hairs with a clear, sticky exudate at their tips.

These curious leaves trap and digest insects.

WHITE WATER LILY Tuberous water lily
Nymphaea tuberosa Paine
Water Lily family   Nymphaeaceae

aquatic   summer   floating

Floating white flowers with concentric rows of tapered petals; outer rings of petals larger than those in center. There is a yellow disk in the center of the blossom.

Leaves are large, flat, round with a deep notch at the base, long-stalked, lower surface green to dull purple.

Flowers not especially fragrant.

WHITE CAMPION or Evening Lychnis
Lychnis alba Mill.
Pink family   Caryophyllaceae

meadows   summer, early fall
18-48 in. (4.5-12 dm)

Flowers have 5 white, deeply notched petals attached to a more or less inflated sac. The thread-like styles are mostly contained within the flower tube, seldom extending beyond the petals. In contrast to Bladder Campion the sac is definitely hairy, usually more tubular than bell-shaped; the sac (calyx) of a mature flower is greenish and usually has green veins but (rarely) these may be reddish-brown; veins are roughly parallel and extend from the base of the calyx (sac) to its tip. Flowers tend to open in the evening.

Leaves are opposite, hairy, 1/2-1 1/2 in. (1-4 cm) long; margins entire.

Stems are hollow and coarsely hairy.

COMMON or NODDING LADIES'-TRESSES
Spiranthes cernua (L.) Rich.
Orchid family   Orchidaceae

bogs, wet meadows   late summer, fall
8-18 in. (20-46 cm)

A terminal spike of nodding white flowers arranged in a double spiral along the central stem.

Leaves mostly at the base of the plant, long (up to 12 in. or 30 cm), very narrow. Stem leaves are greatly reduced in size, sometimes a mere scale-like projection.

PROTECTED MICHIGAN WILDFLOWER
DO NOT DISTURB

CUT-LEAVED WATER-HOREHOUND
Lycopus americanus Muhl.
Mint family   Labiatae

swamps, wet areas   summer, fall
6-24 in. (1.5-6 dm)

Flowers white, tiny, in dense whorled clusters around the stem in leaf axils.

Leaves longer than wide, opposite each other in pairs. Margins of leaves on upper stem are coarsely toothed; tip ends of the lower leaves are similarly coarsely toothed but the portion of the margins closer to the leafstalk are deeply cleft into sharp pointed lobes.

Stems are 4-sided, usually smooth but may be somewhat hairy especially in the area where the leaves attach to the stem so may be concealed by the whorled flowers.

BONESET or Thoroughwort
Eupatorium perfoliatum L.
Composite family   Compositae

bogs, swales, meadows   summer, fall
18 in. - 5 ft. (4.5-15 dm)

Flat-topped clusters of dull white (rarely purple) flowers with 9-23 blossoms in each flower head. Each individual flower appears to be a tuft of rod-like filaments with no apparent petals.

Leaves in pairs opposite each other, broad at base and surrounding the stem so the stem appears to pierce the leaves; slightly fuzzy on the upper surface and even more definitely hairy on the lower surface.

Stem is conspicuously hairy.

Round-leaved Sundew   D

White Water Lily   B

White Campion   C

Common Ladies'-tresses

D

Cut-leaved Water-Horehound

D

Boneset

B

YARROW
Achillea Millefolium L.
Composite family   Compositae

meadows   summer, fall   1-3 ft. (3-9 dm)

Flat-topped flower clusters made up of many, small, individual, 5-petaled blossoms. Usually white but sometimes pinkish.

Leaves are finely cut into many small divisions; increase in size from top to bottom of plant.

Stems are smooth or covered with white-cottony fuzz. Plant has a strong aroma.

FLAT-TOPPED ASTER
Aster umbellatus Mill.
Composite family   Compositae

swales, streambanks, meadows
late summer   2-7 ft. (6-21 dm)

Flat-topped clusters of white, sometimes purple-tinged, few "petaled" (7-14) flowers; individual flowers ½-¾ in. (12-19 mm) across.

Leaves are variable in size but always long and narrow (up to 6 in. (16 cm) long, tapered at each end.

Lower leaves are smaller than upper and soon dry up; stalkless; margins entire but rough to the touch.

WHITE LETTUCE
Prenanthes alba L.
Composite family   Compositae

woods   late summer, fall
18 in. - 5 ft. (4.5-15 dm)

Bell-shaped, drooping, fragrant flowers that are white, yellow-white, or pink with purplish bracts at their bases.

Leaves on lower stem are long-stalked, mostly triangular in outline with variations having 3-5 sharp pointed lobes. Leaves on upper stem are smaller, short-stalked, and more oblong than triangular.

Stems are smooth, stout, and exude milky juice when cut or broken.

GRASS-OF-PARNASSUS
Parnassia glauca Raf.
Saxifrage family   Saxifragaceae

bogs, swamps, meadows   summer, fall
8-20 in. (2-5 dm)

5-petaled white flowers, ¾-1½ in. (2-4 cm) across with distinct, green veins in the petals. Flowers solitary atop a nearly leafless stem. 5 prominent stamens arise between the petals.

Leaves mostly basal with but one small clasping leaf about midway on the stem, margins smooth.

SMALL GRASS-OF-PARNASSUS
P. parviflora DC.   not shown

Smaller than *P. glauca*, the height, leaves, and blossoms being only about half the size. Flowering time commences a little earlier (June).

VIRGIN'S BOWER or Old man's beard
Clematis virginiana L.
Crowfoot family   Ranunculaceae

open woods and edges   summer, early fall   vine

White foamy clusters of flowers whose 4 sepals look like petals.

There are no true petals but the creamy yellow stamens resembling bristles are numerous and conspicuous. Flowers arise from the leaf axils.

Each leaf is composed of 3 leaflets on stalks of approximately equal length but the stalk of the terminal leaflet is slightly longer than the other two. Margins are coarsely toothed, each tooth sharp pointed.

Stems are viny, supported by surrounding vegetation.

Fruits are clusters of seeds, each seed terminated with long 1-2 in. (2.5-5 cm) silky plumes. From this feature comes the name.

WILD CUCUMBER or Balsam-apple
Echinocystis lobata (Michx.) T. & G.
Gourd family   Cucurbitaceae

woods, streambanks
summer, early fall   vine

6-petaled white to greenish-white flowers. Male flowers on elongated, erect stalks from leaf axils; female flowers are also from leaf axils but are fewer, less conspicuous, and on shorter stalks.

Leaves resemble maple leaves with 3-7 but usually 5 sharp pointed, triangular lobes. Leafstalks are about as long as the leaf blade.

Stem is a 4-sided vine climbing on adjacent supports or vegetation by means of string-like forked tendrils.

Fruit is an inflated, greenish bladder, 1-2 in. (2.5-5 cm) long, covered with weak bristles.

Yarrow

A

Grass-of-Parnassus   C

Flat-topped
Aster

C

Virgin's Bower   B

White Lettuce

C

Wild Cucumber   C

MARSH MARIGOLD or Cowslip

Caltha palustris L.
Crowfoot family   Ranunculaceae

swamps, swales, streams   spring
1-2 ft. (3-6 dm)

Conspicuous yellow flowers ½-1½ in. (12-38 mm) across with 5-9 "petals".

Leaves are smooth, shiny, rounded or heart-shaped, as large as a person's hand; indented at base; margins are sawtoothed.

Stems are stout, erect, and hollow.

A plant of wet places, even into shallow water. More likely to be found growing in colonies blanketing rather extensive areas rather than as individual plants.

BUTTERCUP

Ranunculus acris L.
Crowfoot family   Ranunculaceae

wet meadows, swales   spring to fall
2-3 ft. (6-9 dm)

Flowers are yellow with 5-7 glossy, overlapping petals. The bushy stamens are prominent in the center of the flower.

Leaves on the lower stem are divided into 3 segments, each deeply and sharply lobed. Upper leaves are greatly reduced in size and complexity. Leaves are hairy, especially on the lower surface.

Stems are smooth at the upper end but usually very hairy on the lower portion.

YELLOW TROUT LILY

or Adder's tongue
Erythronium americanum Ker.
Lily family   Liliaceae

woods   spring   6-10 in. (15-26 cm)

Flowers yellow, nodding, one per plant; 6 backward curving petals. Back side of petals often purple or brownish-purple. 6 prominent red-brown or yellow anthers extend beyond the bell-shaped blossom.

Leaves 2, at base of plant, often conspicuously mottled with brown. Plants usually found in colonies with many sterile (nonblossoming) plants.

FAWN LILY

E. albidum Nutt.
not shown

This species is closely related to Yellow Trout Lily but the flower is white and the leaves are not mottled. Very rare.

**PLEASE DO NOT PICK
EITHER OF THESE**

LARGE-FLOWERED BELLWORT

Uvularia grandiflora Sm.
Lily family   Liliaceae

woods   spring   8-20 in. (2-5 dm)

6-petaled, bell-shaped, tubular, yellow flowers up to 2 in. (5 cm) long. Blossoms (and leaves) tend to droop as though the plant were wilting.

Leaves are broad and up to 5 in. (13 cm) long, are smooth on the upper surface and faintly fuzzy on the lower; veins are parallel.

Base of leaf clasps the stem to appear as though the stem passes through the leaf.

INDIAN CUCUMBER-ROOT

Medeola virginiana L.
Lily family   Liliaceae

woods   late spring   1-3 ft. (3-9 dm)

Greenish-yellow flowers from tip of plant on long, slender stalks that permit the flowers to dangle beneath the upper whorl of leaves. Petals curve backward. 3 spreading, brownish colored, thread-like styles from top of ovary.

Leaves are in whorls, one whorl of 5-9 midway up stem, a second whorl of 3-5 at top of stem. Leaves are wide but taper to each end.

Fruit is a dark purple berry. Toxicity unknown. Caution!

CLINTONIA or Bluebead lily

Clintonia borealis (Ait.) Raf.
Lily family   Liliaceae

woods, cedar swamps   spring, early summer   6-15 in. (15-38 cm)

Bell-shaped, mostly nodding, yellow to greenish-yellow flowers on a leafless stalk; anthers extend well beyond the petals.

Leaves are thick, broad, essentially oblong, up to 12 in. (3 dm) long and 4 in. (1 dm) wide. Usually 2 or 3 leaves at base of plant but there may be 4; margins are finely hairy; veins are parallel to the midrib. Base of leafstalk sheaths the stem.

Fruit is a blue berry (Aug-Sept). Toxic.

PLEASE DO NOT PICK

yellow

Marsh Marigold   B

Large-flowered Bellwort   C

Buttercup

B

Indian Cucumber-root   D

Yellow
Trout Lily

C

Clintonia

C

55

TUFTED LOOSESTRIFE
Lysimachia thyrsiflora L.
Primrose family   Primulaceae

swales, wet meadows   spring to mid-summer   1-2 ft. (3-6 dm)

Tufts or balls of yellow flowers on short flowerstalks from leaf axils near middle of stem. Numerous projecting stamens that are nearly twice as long as the petals.

Leaves are long, 2-4 in. (5-10 cm), narrow, opposite in pairs.

Stems are erect and hairy.

DOWNY YELLOW VIOLET
Viola pubescens Ait.
Violet family   Violaceae

woods   spring and fall   4-12 in. (1-3 dm)

Yellow, pansy-like flowers at top of stem. Petals have brown-purple lines at their base, the two side petals bearded.

Leaves are on the same stem with flowers, heart-shaped, usually 2-4 on a stem, and there may be 1-2 basal leaves. Leafstalks, veins, and leaf margins are downy.

Stems are also downy, 1 or 2 per plant.

Essentially a spring flowering plant but may rebloom in the fall.

SMOOTH YELLOW VIOLET
V. eriocarpa Schw.
not shown

Has more basal leaves (1-5) than *V. pubescens*. Stems and leaves are smooth or only very sparsely downy.

COREOPSIS or Tickseed
Coreopsis lanceolata L.
Composite family   Compositae

dunes, dry woods, meadows   spring, summer   2-3 ft. (6-9 dm)

Flowers are conspicuously bright yellow, borne singly at tips of long stems. There are 8 "petals" each having 3-7 but usually 4 lobes at its tip. There are 2 sets of bracts at the base of flower.

Leaves are long and narrow and found mainly on the lower part of the plant.

Stems are smooth, tend to stand erect but may be found in a reclining position.

GOLDEN RAGWORT
Senecio aureus L.
Composite family   Compositae

swamps, swales   spring, early summer
1-3 ft. (3-9 dm)

Flowers are on slender stalks forming flat-topped heads. Each of the several flowers is bright yellow, ½-1 in. (12-25 mm) in diameter, with 8-12 "petals" (ray flowers) surrounding a mass of yellow disk flowers. Bracts below the blossom are often purple tipped.

Plant has both basal and stem leaves present. Basal leaves are heart-shaped with blunt tips; leafstalks are long; leaves often reddish on lower surface. Stem leaves are much narrower, deeply cleft into lobes, alternate on the stem, and are stalkless.

COMMON DANDELION
Taraxacum officinale Weber
Composite family   Compositae

meadows, lawns   spring to fall
2-18 in. (5-46 cm)

Flower is borne at the tip of the erect flowerstalk that arises from ground level, is leafless, hollow, exudes a milky juice when cut or broken. The solitary yellow flower head is up to 2 in. (5 cm) wide composed of many tiny individual florets. Calyx is recurved (turns downward away from the petals).

Leaves form a basal rosette, are deeply cleft forming pointed lobes facing downward (toward the base of the leaf).

Seeds are borne in a conspicuous, round, fuzzy ball.

GOAT'S RUE or Rabbit Pea
Tephrosia virginiana (L.) Pers.
Bean family   Fabaceae

dry meadows, woods   early summer
8-20 in. (2-5 dm)

Bicolored red and yellow flowers in clusters at end of main stem or lateral branches.

Leaves pinnately compound; leaflets oval, 8-14 pairs and one terminal leaflet.

Fruit is a very hairy pod 1½-2 in. long (3.5-5.5 cm). Plant is conspicuously covered with soft, light colored hairs.

Tufted Loosestrife   D

Golden Ragwort   B

Common
Dandelion

A

Downy Yellow Violet   C

Coreopsis   A

Goats Rue   C

WOOD BETONY or Lousewort
Pedicularis canadensis L.
Figwort family   Scrophulariaceae

dry woods   late spring
6-16 in. (1.5-4 dm)

Loose clusters of tubular flowers at tips of stems; color often yellow but may be red or combinations of yellow and red. Tubular blossoms flare into 2 lips, the upper one is hood-like and longer than the lower.

Leaves are long, narrow, with deeply notched margins. Most of the leaves are at the base of the plant, but there are some stem leaves and these decrease in size from bottom to top of plant.

Leaves are very hairy and are often red in color.

YELLOW LADY'S-SLIPPER
Cypripedium Calceolus L.
Orchid family   Orchidaceae

swamps, bogs, wet woods   late spring   1-2 ft. (3-6 dm)

Flower is a yellow, inflated pouch, single or sometimes 2 per stem. Petals are long, narrow, twisted, and mottled with brown or purple.

Stem is leafy with 3-6 broad, parallel veined leaves that somewhat sheath the stem.

**PROTECTED MICHIGAN WILDFLOWER
DO NOT DISTURB**

YELLOW WOOD-SORREL
Oxalis stricta L.
Wood-sorrel family   Oxalidaceae

meadows   late spring to fall
prostrate to 18 in. (46 cm)

Yellow, 5-petaled flowers are ¼-½ in. (6-13 mm) across; base of petals may be reddish. Flowerstalks are much longer than leafstalks.

Leaves are clover-like with 3 leaflets radiating from a central point, each with a distinct notch at its tip; dark green in color.

Leaves, leafstalks, and stems may be quite smooth to very hairy. These plants are often found as weeds in lawns and gardens.

SQUAWROOT
Conopholis americana (L.) Wallr.
Broomrape family   Orobanchaceae

dry woods   late spring   3-8 in. (8-20 cm)

Tubular, yellow, stalkless flowers emerging from under compact scales, the flowers and scales together forming a cylindrical spike. Lower scales are overlapping, fleshy, pointed, and yellow to yellow-brown in color.

Plant resembles a yellow colored pine cone standing on end.

Plants usually found in groups. A parasite on tree roots, especially oak.

FALSE HEATHER
Hudsonia tomentosa Nutt.
Rockrose family   Cistaceae

dunes   late spring, early summer
prostrate to 8 in. (20 cm)

Very numerous, 5-petaled yellow flowers, tiny (up to ⅜ in. or 10 mm) wide, mostly at the ends of the branches. Stamens are projecting yellow rods with knobbed tips.

Leaves are tiny, scale-like, overlapping, covered with gray-white hairs.

Stems are prostrate to slightly ascending giving rise to a compact plant form that may be up to 2 ft. (6 dm) across.

HAIRY PUCCOON
Lithospermum caroliniense (Walt.) MacMill.
Borage family   Boraginaceae

dunes, meadows, dry woods   late spring, summer   1-2 ft. (3-6 dm)

Tubular flowers flaring into 5, bright orange-yellow, rounded petals. Flowers up to 1 in. (2.5 cm) across.

Leaves are many, 1-2 in. (3-6 cm) long, much longer than broad, hairy; leaf margins entire but hairy. The numerous leaves are alternate along the stem.

Stems arise from a woody base and become many branched as the season advances.

PLEASE DO NOT PICK

HOARY PUCCOON
L. canescens (Michx.) Lehm.
(not shown)

A related species also found in the area, is similar but smaller than *L. caroliniense*.

Wood Betony   C

Squawroot   D

Yellow
Lady's-slipper

          C

False Heather   C

Yellow Wood-sorrel   C

Hairy
Puccoon

          C

WILD PARSNIP
Pastinaca sativa L.
Parsley family   Umbelliferae

meadows spring to fall 2-5 ft. (0.6-1.5 m)

Flower head is flat-topped made up of open, spreading clusters of individual flowers which are small, yellow, and have 15-25 primary rays ("petals"). Each flower cluster is 2-6 in. (5-15 cm) wide.

Leaves are alternate, pinnately compound with 5-15 leaflets which are so deeply cleft as to appear as many times this number. Leaflets up to 4 in. (10 cm) long, margins sharply toothed and lobed.

Leafstalks clasp the main stem. Both basal and stem leaves present.

Stem is grooved, hairy, erect, and stout.

GOLDEN ALEXANDERS
Zizia aurea (L.) Koch
Parsley family   Umbelliferae

moist meadows spring up to 3 ft. (9 dm)

Compared to *Pastinaca sativa* this plant is usually shorter, rarely exceeding 3 ft. (9 dm) in height. The yellow flowers have fewer primary rays (10-18); the lower leaves may be subdivided into 2 or 3 secondary leafstalks and 3 leaflets on each stalk. It is found in wetter habitats and the flowering period seldom lasts beyond early summer (July). Stems may be reddish and the crushed stems and leaves have a strong parsley odor.

YELLOW PIMPERNEL
Taenidia integerrima (L.) Drude
Parsley family   Umbelliferae

dry woods, meadows   early summer 1-3 ft. (3-9 dm.)

Similar to the two species above but has oval-shaped leaflets that have entire margins. Stems are smooth. Found in drier habitats.

SMOOTHISH HAWKWEED
Hieracium floribundum Wimm. & Grab.
Composite family   Compositae

meadows   summer   8-32 in. (2-8 dm)

Flowerhead is a semi-open to compact cluster of yellow flowers, each about ¾ in. (2 cm) across; "petals" notched at tips; flower bracts with black spines.

Leaves are 1-6 in. (2.5-14 cm) long, narrow (less than 1 in. or 20 mm), and form a basal rosette. There may be 1 or 2 very small stem leaves. Leaves are mostly smooth on the upper surface with only a few hairs near the margin. On the lower surface there are bristles along the midrib; margins are bristly. Stems are sparsely covered with bristles and along with the leaves may have a thin white coating. Roots send out many spreading runners to form new plants (rhizomes).

KING DEVIL
Hieracium florentinum All.
Composite family   Compositae

Similar to *H. floribundum* but the leaves are essentially smooth, there are only a few black hairs on the flower bracts, and runners are not present.

YELLOW HAWKWEED
or Field Hawkweed   not shown
Hieracium pratense Tausch.

meadows, dry woods   late spring, summer   1-3 ft. (3-9 dm)

Flowers are in a more compact cluster than *H. floribundum*. Flower bracts and stems are heavily covered with black, spiny hairs. The basal leaves are hairy on both surfaces. Flowering begins a little earlier in the season. This is a yellow version of Orange Hawkweed, *H. aurantiacum*.

YELLOW ROCKET or Winter cress
Barbarea vulgaris R.Br.
Mustard family   Cruciferae

meadows spring, summer 1-2 ft. (3-6 dm)

4-petaled, elongated clusters of yellow flowers at tips of flowering branches.

Lower leaves are deeply cleft into one large, rounded, terminal lobe and several small, rounded lobes. Upper leaves are coarsely toothed; bases clasp the stem. Fruits are long, narrow seed-pods.

yellow

Wild
Parsnip

A

Smoothish
Hawkweed

A

Golden
Alexanders

C

King
Devil

C

Yellow
Pimpernel

C

Yellow
Rocket

A

61

LEAFY SPURGE
Euphorbia Esula L.
Spurge family   Euphorbiaceae

dunes, meadows   spring to fall
1-2 ft. (3-6 dm)

Flowers are small, greenish-yellow, inconspicuous in themselves but surmounting a pair of prominent yellow bracts that might be mistaken for flowers. Bracts rounded with pointed tips.

Leaves are long, ¾-3 in. (2-8 cm), narrow, few and scattered on lower stem, numerous on upper stem; margins entire.

Stems are erect, smooth, and branched.

GOAT'S-BEARD
Tragopogon dubius Scop.
Composite family   Compositae

meadows   summer, fall   1-3 ft. (3-9 dm)

A solitary, yellow flower head at tip of stem, outer "petals" 5-notched at tip and are exceeded in length by the long, thin, pointed bracts. The flowerstalk below the blossom is inflated and hollow.

Leaves are alternate, grass-like, and clasp the stem.

Stems are smooth, upright, and exude a milky juice when cut or broken. Seed head a large, round, feathery ball.

Hybridizes freely so there are variations. *T. pratensis* L. has bracts that are shorter than the "petals" and the flowerstalk is not inflated. Purple Goatsbeard or Oyster Plant, *T. porrifolius*, is similar to *dubius* but has purple flowers and prefers moister sites.

BUTTERFLY WEED   Orange Milkweed
Asclepias tuberosa L.
Milkweed family   Asclepiacaceae

dunes, meadows   early summer, fall
1-2 ft. (3-6 dm)

Flower clusters are mostly at the top of the stem but occasionally smaller clusters may be found in leaf axils. Color mostly bright orange. Lower part of the flower (calyx) turns backwards (reflexed) which is typical of milkweeds.

Leaves are narrow, 2-4 in. (5-10 cm) long, and covered with soft, short hairs. The margins are entire.

Stems are finely hairy. Unlike other milkweeds this one does not have milky juice.

Seed pods are slender, and smooth.

PLEASE DO NOT PICK

WOOD LILY
Lilium philadelphicum L.
Lily family   Liliaceae

dunes, meadows   early summer
1-3 ft. (3-9 dm)

Flowers are cup-like and upward facing, usually reddish-orange but ranging from yellow (rare) to brilliant red. 6 petals with purplish spots at their base.

Stamens project well beyond the petals. There may be one to several flowers in bloom on the same stem at one time.

Leaves mostly in whorls or circles around the stem with 4-8 in a group (there may be a few single leaves scattered along the stem between the whorls); leaves are long, narrow, sharp pointed.

Stem is stiffly upright bearing the flowers at its tip and covered with a white powdery substance.

PLEASE DO NOT PICK

MICHIGAN LILY
Lilium superbum L.
Lily family   Liliaceae

moist meadows   summer   3-6 ft. (9-18 dm)

One to many nodding, orange to red-orange, showy flowers up to 3 in. (8 cm) across, all at top of plant, each one on its own flowerstalk which may be up to 1 ft. (3 dm) long. 3 petals and 3 petal-like sepals are strongly backcurved so their points almost touch behind the flower. The 6 extended stamens are very conspicuous.

Leaves mostly in a series of whorls up the stem; long, narrow, pointed at each end.

Stems are rigidly upright and smooth.

DAY LILY
Hemerocallis fulva L.
Lily family   Liliaceae

meadows   early summer   3-6 ft. (9-18 dm)

The upward facing, 6-petaled blossom at the tip of the stem is similar to *Lilium philadelphicum*. However, the flower color is more yellowish-orange, the petals are not spotted but do have prominent darker colored streaks (veins) and turn to a yellow color at their base. Rarely is there more than one blossom open at one time and this lasts for just a day. Flowerstalk is leafless.

Leaves are basal, ½-¾ths the length of the flowerstalk and usually less than 1½ in. (4 cm) wide.

Leafy Spurge

B

Wood Lily   B

Michigan Lily

B

Goat's-beard   B

Day Lily

B

Butterfly Weed   B

63

BLACK-EYED SUSAN or Coneflower
Rudbeckia hirta L.
Composite family   Compositae

meadows   summer, fall   1-3 ft. (3-9 dm)

Large, conspicuous flowers with yellow to yellow-orange "petals" which are often darker color near their base. Central disk is brown, sometimes purplish, rarely yellow, and is domed.

Leaves are much longer than broad, very hairy.

Stems are very hairy, erect, and stout.

ORANGE HAWKWEED or
Devil's paintbrush
Hieracium aurantiacum L.
Composite family   Compositae

meadows   summer   8-24 in. (2-6 dm)

Orange to reddish-orange flowers about ⅜-¾ in. (1-2 cm) across in a crowded cluster at the top of the single stem.

Leaves are at the base of the plant and there may be 1 or 2 greatly reduced leaves on the stem; leaves very hairy both surfaces.

Stem is very hairy and contains milky juice particularly at the base.

Plants usually occur in extensive colonies and may cover entire fields and meadows.

SPOTTED JEWELWEED
or Touch-me-not
Impatiens biflora Walt.
Touch-me-not family   Balsaminaceae

swales, wet meadows   summer, early fall   2-5 ft. (6-15 dm)

Dangling, single, orange colored blossoms with flaring red to brownish spotted petals and a prominent spur at rear that curves back under the flower. Flowers are about 1 in. (2.5 cm) long.

Leaves smooth, thin, long-stalked, egg-shaped with rounded teeth on the margins.

Stems smooth, succulent, freely branched, exuding watery juice when broken, Swollen at lower leaf joints.

Mature seed pods burst suddenly when touched.

MONEYWORT
Lysimachia Nummularia L.
Primrose family   Primulaceae

swales, wet meadows summer prostrate

Single yellow flowers on long flowerstalks from leaf axils, 1 in. (2-3 cm) across; 5 petals dotted with dark red.

Leaves in pairs along the creeping stem, are round in shape, and have entire margins.

SILVERWEED
Potentilla Anserina L.
Rose family   Rosaceae

moist meadows   summer   prostrate

Usually 5-petaled (sometimes 6 or more) yellow flowers up to 1 in. (2.5 cm) across on leafless stalks. Each petal and the entire flower is essentially round.

Leaves are pinnately compound with 7 to many leaflets which are somewhat hairy on the upper surface but with prominent, long, silvery hairs beneath (from which the plant derives its name); margins coarsely and sharply toothed. Leaflets are larger at the terminal end of the leaf and are interspersed with much smaller leaflets.

Plants spread by runners that are usually red and long hairy.

SULFUR CINQUEFOIL
or Rough-Fruited Cinquefoil
Potentilla recta L.
Rose family   Rosaceae

meadows   summer   1-2 ft. (3-6 dm)

Pale, delicate, yellow flowers with 5 petals, each with a rounded notch at its outer margin. Center of flower is a darker yellow disk.

Leaves at the base and on the lower stem are long-stalked, terminating in 5-7 long, narrow, toothed leaflets that are hairy on both surfaces. Higher on the stem the leaflets are short-stalked or stalkless, much smaller, and may be only 3 in number.

Stems are stout, hairy, and erect.

Black-eyed
Susan

A

Moneywort   D

Orange Hawkweed   A

Silverweed   C

Spotted Jewelweed   C

Sulfur Cinquefoil   B

65

SMOOTH SOWTHISTLE
Sonchus uliginosus Bieb.
Composite family   Compositae

meadows summer, fall up to 4 ft. (1.2 m)

Yellow, dandelion-like flowers at ends of upper stems; 1¼-2 in. (3-5 cm) across; "petals" many, and narrow, blunt ended with multiple notched tips; flowerstalks and sepals are smooth.

Leaves alternate, mostly on lower half of stem; larger lower leaves with 2-5 (occasionally 7) lobes each side of midrib. Upper leaves mostly unlobed. Base of leaf clasps stem with rounded, prickly, ear-like projections. Leaf margins soft-spiny.

Stems stout, erect, hollow, and contain milky juice.

EVENING PRIMROSE
Oenothera biennis L.
Evening Primrose family   Onagraceae

dunes, dry woods, meadows   summer, fall   2-5 ft. (6-15 dm)

Flowers have 4 broad, yellow petals. There is a cross-shaped structure (stigma) in the center of the flower. Blossoms tend to open late in the day and wilt the next day. The 4 long-pointed, swept-back sepals often appear as only 2.

Leaves are stalkless, 4-8 in. (10-20 cm) long, narrow, smooth to very slightly hairy; leaf margins vary from smooth to a few widely spaced very small teeth.

Stems are stout, upright, reddish in the lower portion, and downy to slightly bristly.

Fruit is a long, narrow capsule with the cross-shaped stigma often still attached to its tip.

AGRIMONY
Agrimonia gryposepala Wallr.
Rose family   Rosaceae

woods and edges   summer
up to 5 ft. (15 dm)

Small, 5-petaled, yellow, wedge-shaped flowers borne on a narrow spike which is often curved. Short flowerstalks flare into a bell-shaped calyx tube beneath the petals.

Leaves are pinnately compound with 5-9 comparatively large, equal size leaflets with tiny, variable shaped leaflets interspersed. Margins of larger leaflets coarsely and bluntly toothed. Conspicuous

stipules (leaf-like appendages) are found at the base of the leafstalk and surround the hairy stem.

Fruit is a conical-shaped bur with hooked bristles on its upper (flattened) end; sticks to clothing.

YELLOW PONDLILY or Bullhead lily
Nuphar variegatum Engelm.
Water Lily family   Nymphaeaceae

ponds, still water   summer   aquatic

Cup-like yellow flowers just above the surface of ponds and quiet, shallow water; a large, yellow disk (stigma) in center.

Large, round, floating leaves have a narrow notch at the base of the blade; leafstalks are submerged, smooth, flexible, and flattened on the upper side.

SWAMP CANDLE or Yellow Loosestrife
Lysimachia terrestris (L.) BSP.
Primrose family   Primulaceae

wet meadows, wet woods   summer
12-30 in. (3-7.5 dm)

Single spike of open to rather densely clustered 5-petaled, yellow flowers at top of plant. Base of petals marked with dark (usually reddish) spots or broken lines.

Leaves are paired and opposite, long and narrow, margins entire.

Mature plants often have reddish bulblets in leaf axils.

Stem is smooth, upright, and although it may be branched, usually has a single flowering spike.

COMMON ST. JOHN'S-WORT
Hypericum perforatum L.
St. John's-wort family   Hypericaceae

meadows   summer, early fall
12-30 in. (3-7.5 dm)

Flowers are yellow, numerous, about 1 in. (2.5 cm) across, 5 petals, and many prominent bushy stamens from the center. Many black dots occur along the margins of the petals (a hand lens is useful in seeing these).

Leaves are in pairs and opposite each other, stalkless and toothless. Tiny transluscent dots on leaves may be seen by holding a leaf up to the light.

Stems are smooth and many branched.

Smooth Sowthistle

B

Yellow Pondlily   B

Swamp
Candle

B

Evening Primrose   B

Agrimony

C

Common St. John's-wort   A

GROUND CHERRY
Physalis heterophylla Nees.
Nightshade family   Solanaceae

meadows summer, early fall 1-3 ft. (3-9 dm)

Bell-shaped flowers borne singly from the leaf axils. Petals are light yellow and become a darker color at their base. Calyx and flowerstalks are very hairy.

Leaves are 1-3 in. (2-8 cm) long, pointed at the tips, broadly rounded at the base; margins are smooth or slightly wavy. Leafstalks and upper and lower leaf surfaces are fuzzy. Leaves often have ragged holes caused by insect feeding.

Stems are very hairy and may be sticky to the touch.

Fruit is a berry enclosed in the inflated, yellow-green sac.

Flowers and fruits commonly on the plant at the same time.

Ripe berries are supposedly edible but are rather tasteless and seedy. Unripe berries are poisonous, use caution.

BUTTER-AND-EGGS
Linaria vulgaris Hill.
Figwort family   Scrophulariaceae

meadows summer, fall 12-32 in. (3-8 dm)

Flowers are many on an upright spike; yellow with an orange color marking near the center of the blossom; there is a thin, long-pointed spur at the base. Each flower is about 1 in. (2.5 cm) long including the spur.

Leaves are very numerous, pale green, long, narrow, and pointed at both ends.

Plants spread by underground runners forming colonies of individual plants.

COMMON MULLEIN or Aaron's Rod
Verbascum Thapsus L.
Figwort family   Scrophulariaceae

meadows   summer, early fall   3-6 ft. (9-18 dm)

A long, upright spike at the tip of the stem bears the flower buds and scattered, open, yellow flowers with 5 rounded petals.

Although only a few flowers appear at one time the flowering period extends through the entire summer to fall season.

Leaves are thick and woolly, largest at the base of the plant and getting progressively smaller higher on the stem.

Stem is tall, erect, stout, and densely woolly.

BIRDSFOOT TREFOIL
Lotus corniculatus L.
Bean family   Fabaceae

meadows   summer, fall   prostrate to 2 ft. (6 dm)

Yellow, pea-shaped flowers in clusters of 3-6 at ends of stems.

Compound leaves with 5 leaflets, 3 in clover-like fashion at the end of the leafstalk and 2 more at its base.

Fruits are long, narrow capsules (pods) radiating from a central point giving appearance of a many toed bird's foot.

A crop found in farm fields from which it has escaped to roadsides and other non-cultivated areas. Most prevalent in the eastern Upper Peninsula.

PINESAP
Monotropa Hypopithys L.
Heath family   Ericaceae

woods   summer, fall   4-12 in. (1-3 dm)

A cluster of 3-10 nodding, pale yellow, tan, or reddish (but never white) flowers from tip of a single stem.

Leaves are scale-like, pressed close to stem, and are the same color as the flowers.

Stem is fleshy and soft.

A saprophytic plant deriving its food from woodland humus.

Usually associated with oak trees and sometimes with pine trees.

HORSEMINT
Monarda punctata L.
Mint family   Labiatae

dunes, meadows   summer, fall 1-3 ft. (3-9 dm)

A ring (whorl) of yellow, 2-lipped flowers spotted with purple emerging from a tubed, green calyx above another ring of whitish or purplish bracts (modified leaves). There is usually more than one ring of flowers per stem. The upper lip of each flower is strongly arched.

Leaves are ¾-3 in. (2-8 cm) long, narrow, somewhat fuzzy, occur in pairs with another pair of much smaller leaves at their base.

Stems are erect, square in cross section (4-sided), covered with fine fuzz.

Ground Cherry   C

Birdsfoot Trefoil   A

Butter-and-eggs   A

Pinesap   D

Common Mullein   B

Horsemint   D

WOODLAND SUNFLOWER
Helianthus divaricatus L.
Composite family   Compositae

wood edges, meadows   summer,
early fall   2-5 ft. (6-15 dm)

Flowers are large, 1½-3 in. (4-8 cm) across,
showy yellow, with 8-15 "petals" which
are long and narrow. Blossoms may be
solitary or few per stem but occasionally
are numerous. Center of flower is yellow.

Leaves are mostly paired and opposite;
either stalkless or with very short stalks;
rough on the upper surface and hairy on
the lower; length is 2-6 in. (5-15 cm) and
up to 3 in. (8 cm) wide.

Stems are smooth and often covered
with a grayish, waxy coating.

TALL or GREEN-HEADED CONEFLOWER
Rudbeckia laciniata L.
Composite family   Compositae

swamps, moist meadows   summer,
fall   3-10 ft. (1-3 m.)

Flowers 2½-4 in. (6-16 cm.) wide with
6-10 recurved (drooping) "petals"
(rayflowers). Center of flower is a globe-
shaped greenish-yellow knob that usually
elongates as the flower matures. There is
a single flower on each flowerstalk.

Leaves are single, entire to 3-lobed in
upper part of plant; lower leaves are
pinnately compound with 5-7 irregularly
toothed leaflets.

Stems are woody at the base; smooth.

TALL SUNFLOWER
Helianthus giganteus L.
Composite family   Compositae

swamps, moist meadows   late
summer, fall   4-10 ft. (1.2-3m.)

Flowers 2-3 in. (5-7.5 cm.) across, sometimes single but usually several; 10-20
yellow "petals" (rayflowers). Central
disk flowers are yellow to brownish.
Flower bracts are long and pointed.
Leaves are simple, have pointed tips,
are alternate along the upper stem but
may be opposite on the lower stem.
Upper leaf surface is rough and the
lower surface is finely hairy. Margins
are entire to shallow-toothed.

Stems are rough and hairy and often
reddish.

CANADA GOLDENROD
Solidago canadensis L.
Composite family   Compositae

meadows   summer, fall   1-5 ft. (3-15 dm)

Feathery plumes of tiny yellow flowers
at tip of stem.

There are many leaves that are long,
narrow, smooth, with coarsely sawtoothed margins. Midrib and veins on
lower leaf suface may be hairy.

Stem is smooth near the bottom, notice-
ably downy in upper part.

BLUESTEM GOLDENROD
Solidago caesia L.
Composite family   Compositae

woods and edges   late summer, fall
1-3 ft. (3-9 dm)

Tufts of tiny yellow flowers attached to
the main stem at points where leaves are
also attached (leaf axils).

Leaves are long, narrow, stalkless, taper
to a pointed tip; surfaces are usually
smooth but may have a few short hairs
along the veins; margins are entire to
sawtoothed.

Stems are smooth, usually with a blue or
purple coating which can be rubbed off.

COMMON TANSY
Tanacetum vulgare L.
Composite family   Compositae

meadows   summer, fall   1-4 ft. (3-12 dm)

A flat-topped cluster of many, bright
yellow flower heads, ¼-¾ in. (5-10 mm)
across; formed only at tip of stem.
Flowers appear to have no petals thus
resemble yellow buttons.

Leaves are alternate, deeply cut (almost
to the midrib), lobes with sawtooth margins, surfaces smooth or nearly so.

Stems mostly smooth and ridged. An
aromatic but poisonous plant if ingested.

HURON TANSY
T. huronense Nutt.
not shown

Similar to T. vulgare but flowers are
fewer, larger, and may have very short,
inconspicuous "petals"; leaves and stems
are hairy.

Habitat is more closely related to the
beaches along the northern Great Lakes.

**A THREATENED SPECIES
DO NOT DISTURB**

Woodland
Sunflower

B

Canada
Goldenrod

B

Tall Coneflower   B

Bluestem
Goldenrod

C

Tall
Sunflower

B

Common
Tansy

A

BROADLEAF SPRING BEAUTY
Claytonia caroliniana Michx.
Purslane family   Portulacaceae

woods   spring   6-10 in. (15-26 cm)

Usually 5-petaled pink or white flowers conspicuously marked with dark pink veins; style is 3-parted; there are 2 green sepals.

A single pair of smooth leaves halfway up the stem (rarely there may be 3 leaves), oval in shape, 1-3 in. (2-8 cm) long, with a definite leafstalk.

Leaves are thick and succulent.

Occurs primarily in the northern part of the State.

SPRING BEAUTY
Claytonia virginica L.
Purslane family   Portulacaceae

Distinguish from *C. caroliniana* by the much longer, 3-7 in. (7-18 cm) and narrower leaves which are stalkless, or nearly so. Also, it is more apt to be found in the lower half of Michigan.

ROUND-LOBED HEPATICA or Liverleaf
Hepatica americana (DC.) Ker.
Crowfoot family   Ranunculaceae

woods   spring   4-6 in. (10-15 cm)

Delicate, pink, white, lavender, or blue flowers with 2-10 "petals".

Usually many individual flowers per plant, each with many thread-like stamens in its center, and each borne single on a very hairy flowerstalk; 3 hairy bracts that resemble sepals below each blossom.

Leaves are smooth with 3 rounded lobes; leaves persist through the winter. At blossom time these overwintered leaves are present and have a brown-purple color. New green leaves develop after blossom time.

SHARP-LOBED HEPATICA
H. acutiloba DC.
not shown

Very similar to *H. americana* with these differences:

Leaf lobes are more pointed

Leaves are somewhat larger,

Hairs on flowerstalk are longer, and

Leaves may have 3 or up to 7 lobes.

COLUMBINE or Rock Bells
Aquilegia canadensis L.
Crowfoot family   Ranunculaceae

dry woods, bogs, meadows   spring, early summer   up to 3 ft. (9 dm)

Flowers reddish with yellow centers, hanging or nodding at the end of a graceful, slender stem. The 5 petals have long tubes extending upward (or backward) into 5 curving spurs.

The basal leaves are long-stalked, divided and then divided again into segments of 3. Stem leaves are similar but are stalkless, decreasing in size toward the top of the plant. Leaflets are in 3's.

PLEASE DO NOT PICK

RED WINDFLOWER
Anemone multifida Poir.
Crowfoot family   Ranunculaceae

dunes   late spring, early summer   up to 12 in. (3 dm)

Flowers single, ¾-2 in. (2-5 cm) across, usually red (rarely purple, white, or yellow).

Basal leaves are long-stalked, deeply 3-parted into long, narrow segments. Stem leaves are similar but usually stalkless and occur near the middle of the stem.

Stems are stout, erect, and silky hairy.

Fruit appears as a tuft of cotton atop a long, dried stem.

INDIAN PAINTBRUSH or Painted Cup
Castilleja coccinea (L.) Spreng.
Figwort family   Scrophulariaceae

moist meadows, shores   spring, early fall   1-2 ft. (3-6 dm)

Conspicuous are the red, orange, or scarlet-tipped bracts that conceal the tiny, yellow or greenish true flowers.

Leaves are hairy; those on the stem may be entire (rare) but are usually deeply cleft into 3-5 narrow lobes. In either case the leaves are stalkless. Basal leaves form a rosette.

Stems are upright, often purple, and densely hairy. A parasite on other plants.

Broadleaf Spring Beauty   C

Columbine   C

Red
Windflower

C

Spring Beauty   C

Round-lobed Hepatica   C

Indian
Paintbrush

B

RAM'S-HEAD LADY'S-SLIPPER
Cypripedium arietinum R.Br.
Orchid family   Orchidaceae

woods, swamps, bogs   spring
6-12 in. (15-30 cm)

A single, nodding, pouch-like flower at top of stem. Pouch is conical, sagging on lower side, lined with fine hairs, and marked with darker color veins; pouch is basically white surmounted by a purplish hood.

Leaves are broad (up to 1 in. or 2.5 cm) wide, long pointed, parallel veined, clasp the stem, and only 3-5 per stem; margins are entire.

A small plant difficult to find even though it often grows in colonies. Name from ram's-head appearance of the flower.

**PROTECTED MICHIGAN WILDFLOWER
DO NOT DISTURB**

ARETHUSA or Dragon's Mouth
Arethusa bulbosa L.
Orchid family   Orchidaceae

swamps, bogs   late spring,
early summer   6-12 in. (15-30 cm)

A solitary flower at tip of stem has 3 upright, pink sepals and a matching color hood over the lower lip which is broad, purple spotted, and yellow bearded.

Stem is usually leafless at blossom time. Later, a single, narrow, grass-like leaf appears on the stem.

**PROTECTED MICHIGAN WILDFLOWER
DO NOT DISTURB**

CALYPSO or Fairy Slipper
Calypso bulbosa (L.) Oakes
Orchid family   Orchidaceae

swamps, wet woods   late spring,
early summer   3-8 in. (8-20 cm)

A solitary pink to purple, nodding, slipper-shaped flower at tip of stem. Long, yellow hairs form the "laces" for the slipper.

There are 2 yellow, pointed projections at "toe" of slipper.

Sepals and petals flare outward above the slipper. Dark lines and spots throughout the blossom.

A single, broad bladed, parallel veined leaf at base of the plant.

**A THREATENED SPECIES
DO NOT DISTURB**

SHOWY ORCHIS
Orchis spectabilis L.
Orchid family   Orchidaceae

woods   late spring   4-12 in. (10-30 cm)

Flowers are in an open spike of 3-8 bicolored blossoms; a broad, white lip below an arching pink to red-purple hood formed by sepals and side petals. Flowers have a green, leaf-like bract at their base which is about the length of the blossom.

A pair of long, up to 7 in. (18 cm), smooth, parallel veined leaves are at base of plant; leaves sheath the stem; margins smooth.

**PROTECTED MICHIGAN WILDFLOWER
DO NOT DISTURB**

PINK LADY'S-SLIPPER
or Moccasin flower
Cypripedium acaule Ait.
Orchid family   Orchidaceae

dry woods, swamps, bogs   late spring,
early summer   8-18 in. (20-46 cm)

Flower is a dark to very light, delicate pink; a nodding, inflated pouch or "slipper" with conspicuously darker veins.

The 2 leaves (rarely 3) found at the ground line are very broad, and have parallel veins. Both surfaces are hairy to downy.

One of the commonest orchids. Often found in colonies.

**PROTECTED MICHIGAN WILDFLOWER
DO NOT DISTURB**

ROSE POGONIA
Pogonia ophioglossoides (L.) Ker.
Orchid family   Orchidaceae

bogs, wet meadows   summer
4-20 in. (1-5 dm)

A solitary (rarely 2) flower(s) at tip of stem, pale to deep pink.

Sepals and petals are alike. The bearded and fringed lower lip is the most distinguishing chacteristic along with the green, leaf-like bract that occurs just below the flower.

A single leaf midway on the stem (may be 2-3) that is long and comparatively narrow but too wide to be called grass-like. Base of leaf sheaths the stem.

**PROTECTED MICHIGAN WILDFLOWER
DO NOT DISTURB**

Ram's-head
Lady's-slipper

D

Showy
Orchis

D

Arethusa

D

Pink
Lady's-slipper

C

Calypso

D

Rose
Pogonia

D

RED TRILLIUM or Stinking Benjamin
Trillium erectum L.
Lily family   Liliaceae

woods   spring   6-24 in. (1.5-6 dm)

Flower color usually red to maroon but may vary to purple, yellow, greenish, or white; 1¼-2¾ in. (3-7 cm) across. The single flower is borne above the leaves and has an unpleasant odor.

Sepals are about the same length as the petals.

Leaves are in a whorl, 3 in number.

Stems are upright with a single flower.

**PROTECTED MICHIGAN WILDFLOWER
DO NOT DISTURB**

ROSE TWISTED STALK
or Rose Mandarin
Streptopus roseus Michx.
Lily family   Liliaceae

woods   spring, early summer
1-2 ft. (3-6 dm)

Pink to rose-purple, bell-shaped flowers with 6 lobes, dangling singly on a bent or twisted, hairy flowerstalk that, in turn, arises from the stem at the leaf axil.

Leaves are stalkless, alternate, parallel veined, and have finely hairy margins.

Stem is arched and finely fuzzy.

Fruit is a globular, bright red berry.

WHITE TWISTED STALK
S. amplexifolius (L.) DC.
not shown

Similar to *S. roseus* but flowers are greenish-white or sometimes purple. Leaf bases clasp the stem. Fruit is an elongated, red berry.

PALE CORYDALIS
Corydalis sempervirens (L.) Pers.
Fumitory family   Fumariaceae

rocky meadows   spring to fall
6-24 in. (1.5-6 dm)

Open clusters of pink flowers with bright yellow tips; occur at tip of stem; tube-shaped, ⅜-¾ in. (1-2 cm) in length with the flowerstalk attached at the side of the flower. 4 petals at the end of the tube.

Leaves are alternate, pinnately compound; leaflets mostly 3-lobed, ½ in. (13 mm) in length; lower leaves are stalked, upper are stalkless.

Stems are both upright and prostrate; smooth.

Fruit is a long, narrow, bean-like pod.

WILD GERANIUM or Spotted cranesbill
Geranium maculatum L.
Geranium family   Geraniaceae

woods, meadows   spring, early summer
1-2 ft. (3-6 dm)

Attractive pink, rose-purple, blue, or white flowers, singly or few flowered clusters at end of hairy flowerstalks. Flowers up to 1½ in. (4 cm) across. The 5 petals usually have dark lines (veins).

Leaves palmately compound, 3-5 lobes that are irregularly and coarsely toothed at their tips. Leaves are long-stalked at base of plant, shorter as they get higher on the stem.

Stems are hairy, erect, several to a plant.

Fruit is a long, thin pod resembling a crane's bill.

HERB-ROBERT or Red Robin
Geranium Robertianum L.
Geranium family   Geraniaceae

woods and edges   late spring, summer
10-18 in. (26-46 cm)

Flowers are pink to reddish-purple (rarely white), approximately 12 mm across, with 5 petals that are prominently marked with dark colored streaks. Flowers are usually in pairs on hairy flowerstalks.

Leaves are fern-like, deeply cut into 3-5 segments (leaflets) which, in turn, are deeply cleft.

Stems are erect and hairy, often reddish in color.

Plant is strong scented, the basis for a common name used in England, Stinking Bob.

PITCHER PLANT
Sarracenia purpurea L.
Pitcher plant family   Sarraceniaceae

bogs, marshes, swamps   late spring,
early summer   12-18 in. (3-5 dm)

Dark purple-red, single, nodding, globe-shaped flowers. There are 5 petals folded inward to form the globe.

Leaves are only at the base of the plant, tubular to urn-shaped, hollow, and usually containing water and dead insects. Color of leaves is variable from green to red with yellow stripes and blotches.

Stems are smooth, upright, leafless, and bent over at the tip from weight of the blossom.

**A THREATENED SPECIES
DO NOT DISTURB**

Red Trillium　　D

Wild Geranium　　C

Rose Twisted Stalk　　D

Herb-Robert　　C

Pitcher Plant

Pale Corydalis　　C

C

FRINGED POLYGALA or Gaywings
Polygala paucifolia Willd.
Milkwort family   Polygalaceae

woods, swamps   late spring, early summer   3-6 in. (8-15 cm)

Petals form a tube which is tipped with a delicate fringe. A pink to purple "wing" is on each side of this tube. Blossoms resemble an orchid but there is no relationship.

There are 3-6 oval leaves near the top of the stem with small, scale-like leaves on the lower stem. Stem is tough and woody.

SHOWY LADY'S-SLIPPER
Cypripedium reginae Walt.
Orchid family   Orchidaceae

swamps, bogs, wet woods   early summer   1-3 ft. (3-9 dm)

Flower is a pink and white ball-shaped pouch surmounted with widespreading white sepals and petals. May be up to 3 flowers on separate flowerstalks atop one single stem.

Leaves occur full length of the stem, are alternate, broad (up to 4 in. or one dm wide), veins parallel and prominent; upper and lower surfaces downy; bases clasp the stem.

Stems are erect and hairy. Plants often found in colonies.

PROTECTED MICHIGAN WILDFLOWER DO NOT DISTURB

GRASS PINK
Calopogon pulchellus (Sw.) R.Br.
Orchid family   Orchidaceae

bogs, swamps, meadows   early summer   12-20 in. (3-5 dm)

An open cluster of pink to lavender, rarely white flowers that approximate 1 in. (2.5 cm) across. Petals and sepals mostly similar so blossoms appear to have 5 spreading "petals" and the exception is the single, upright, bearded "lip" at the top of the blossom.

General appearance of the flower is an equal sided triangle.

There may be up to 12 blossoms per plant but usually 2-4.

A single, narrow, grass-like leaf from near the base of the plant, usually 4-8 in. (10-20 cm) long, upright (parallel with stem).

PROTECTED MICHIGAN WILDFLOWER DO NOT DISTURB

RACEMED MILKWORT
Polygala polygama Walt.
Milkwort family   Polygalaceae

dry woods, meadows   summer   to 18 in. (4.5 dm.)

Pink to rose-purple (seldom white) flowers in a loose spike at end of stems. Each flower with a central tube and 2 spreading wings similar to Fringed Polygala.

Leaves are simple, many, alternate, much longer than wide.

There are many stems from a common root, stems smooth, mostly upright but some tendency for outer stems to recline.

TWINFLOWER
Linnaea borealis L.
Honeysuckle family   Caprifoliaceae

wet woods, bogs   early summer   3-5 in. (8-13 cm)

Pale pink, nodding, elongated bell-shaped, fragrant flowers, ½ in. (13 mm) long, usually in pairs from the tip of the flower-stalks which are erect, usually 3-4 in. (8-10 cm) high.

Leaves are in pairs, essentially round, with some rounded teeth at the tip end; remain green year round.

Stems are woody and creep along the ground. Usually found in colonies that form mats.

PLEASE DO NOT PICK

EVERLASTING PEA
Lathyrus latifolius L.
Bean family   Fabaceae

meadows   late spring, summer   climber to 7 ft. (2 m)

Flowers pink, ranging from white to purple, resemble the cultivated sweet pea of the garden; 4-10 showy blossoms in a cluster near the tip of the smooth flowerstalk which may be up to 7 in. (18 cm) long.

There are 2 leaflets from the end of each winged leafstalk. There may be one to several forked tendrils from the tip of the leafstalk. There is a pair of stipules (small leaf-like appendages) at the base of each leafstalk each of them 2-lobed, each lobe very narrow but one is much longer than the other.

Stems are climbing or prostrate. Stems are prominently winged like the leafstalks.

Fringed
Polygala

C

Racemed Milkwort   C

Showy
Lady's-slipper

C

Twinflower   D

Grass Pink

C

Everlasting Pea   B

CROWN VETCH
Coronilla varia L.
Bean family   Fabaceae

meadows late spring, early fall creeper*

Rounded clusters of clover-like, bicolored (pink and white) flowers on long stalks that arise in leaf axils.

Pinnately compound leaves with paired, oval leaflets, usually 11 in number but may be up to 25.

*Stems are reclining or prostrate. A sprawling, many stemmed plant often planted to stabilize soil on steep slopes and road cuts.

Fruit is a long, slender pod.

BEACH PEA
Lathyrus maritimus (L.) Bigel.
Bean family   Fabaceae

dunes, sandy beaches   summer
1-2 ft. (3-6 dm)

A cluster of 3-10 pea flowers on a long flowerstalk, each blossom ¾-1 in. (2-2.5 cm) long; range in color from a delicate pink through purple.

Leaves are pinnately compound with up to 6 pairs of egg-shaped leaflets. A pair of very large stipules is found at the base of the leafstalk. A forked tendril is at the tip of the leafstalk.

Stems are arching, climbing, or only somewhat erect, smooth, angled.

SMALL CRANBERRY
Vaccinium Oxycoccos L.
Heath family   Ericaceae

bogs   early summer   creeping

Flowers have 4 flaring, backward curving, delicate pink lobes united at their base. Reproductive structures are compressed into a protruding, narrow column resembling a bird's beak. The 2-4 in. (5-10 cm) upright flowerstalks are red, fuzzy, and arise from the ends of the prostrate stems; there are usually 2 bracts below the middle of these upright stalks.

Leaves are alternate, pointed-oval in shape, up to ½ in. (1.3 cm) in length, whitish beneath, edges rolled inward.

Stems are reddish, prostrate, trailing, and woody.

Fruit is a rounded, red berry, ¼ in. (6-8 mm) in diameter. Edible but tart.

RED CLOVER
Trifolium pratense L.
Bean family   Fabaceae

meadows   spring-fall   to 24 in. (6 dm.)

Deep purplish-red flowers form a globose, stalkless head at end of branches. Color may vary to almost white. Fragrant.

Leaves are palmately compound with 3 leaflets which usually have a V-shaped, lighter colored design on the blade. Leafstalks very hairy.

Stem is decidedly hairy. An important agricultural plant used for hay and pasture.

PIPSISSEWA or Prince's Pine
Chimaphila umbellata (L.) Bart.
Heath family   Ericaceae

dry woods summer 6-12 in. (15-30 cm)

Flowers are waxy, pale pink or white; spreading clusters nod from tip of stem; 2-8 blossoms per plant, each about ¾ in. (20 mm) across; 5 rounded and concave petals. A ring of red to rose-violet anthers around the green center of the flower.

Leaves are in whorls, 2-3 tiers per stem; dark green, shiny on the upper surface, and sharply toothed along the margins; leaves remain green year-round.

**PROTECTED MICHIGAN WILDFLOWER
DO NOT DISTURB**

PINK PYROLA
Pyrola asarifolia Michx.
Heath family   Ericaceae

woods, swamps summer 6-12 in. (15-30 cm)

A spike of pink to pale purple, nodding, waxy, 5-petaled blossoms.

Pistil exceeds length of the petals.

Leaves basal, kidney-shaped to round, leathery, often shiny. Length of leafstalk exceeds length of leaf blade.

Stem is essentially naked but has one or more scale-like bracts.

LARGE CRANBERRY
Vaccinium macrocarpon Ait.
not shown

Similar to *V. Oxycoccus* but somewhat larger; leaves are more oval and less pointed. Flowerstalks arise along the stem as well as from the tip. The pair of bracts on the flowerstalks are usually above the middle and are green. The plants grow in the same habitat and may be intermixed. Fruit of this species is the one grown commercially.

Crown Vetch   B

Red Clover   B

Beach Pea   C

Pipsissewa

D

Small Cranberry   D

Pink Pyrola

D

DAME'S ROCKET or Sweet Rocket
Hesperis matronalis L.
Mustard family   Cruciferae

meadows, wood edges
spring, midsummer   3-4 ft. (9-12 dm)

Open clusters of pink, white, or purple, 4-petaled, stalked flowers about 1 in. (2.5 cm) across; sepals hairy. Fragrant.

Leaves are alternate, short-stalked or stalkless, definitely not indented at the base; upper surface is finely downy, lower surface with branched hairs; margins may be smooth to undulating but more likely are finely toothed. Blade is 3-4 times longer than broad.

There may be one to many very hairy stems, hairiness increasing from top to bottom of stem.

Fruit is a long (up to 5 in. or 14 cm) cylindrical capsule.

HONESTY or Moonwort or Money Plant
Lunaria annua L.   Cruciferae

Another purple, sometimes white, 4-petaled flower of the Mustard family similar to *Hesperis matronalis* but with these differences:

Stems are not as hairy, blooms earlier in the spring (fading about the time that Dame's Rocket is coming into bloom). Leaf blades are only about twice as long as broad, tapering to a point at the tip, are indented at their base, and are coarsely toothed. Most leaves are alternate but there may be some opposite leaves on the lower stem; very sparsely hairy on both surfaces. Fruits are round, flat, transluscent disks about the size of a silver dollar. Popular in winter bouquets.

WILD BERGAMOT
Monarda fistulosa L.
Mint family   Labiatae

meadows   summer   2-4 ft. (6-12 dm)

Single clusters of tubular pink to lilac colored individual flowers that make a flower head at the tip of the stem. Each tubed flower has a tuft of long hairs at its tip.

Leaves are in pairs, short-stalked, longer than broad, widest below the midpoint, smooth to slightly hairy; margins are toothed.

Stems are also smooth to softly hairy, square in cross section (4-sided).

WILD THYME
Thymus Serpyllum L.
Mint family   Labiatae

dry woods, meadows   summer
up to 12 in. (3 dm)

Flowers very small, pink to purple, form whorled clusters near the tip of the stem, appear to be 4-lobed. Calyx is green with white stripes, minutely hairy. Flowerstalks are short from upper leaf axils.

Leaves are paired, each leaf often with 2 small leaf-like appendages at its base; margins are entire; minute pits are apparent on lower leaf surface.

Stems are 4-angled, finely fuzzy on the angles, mostly woody in the lower portion. Mostly prostrate, forming mats.

WILD BASIL or Dogmint
Satureja vulgaris (L.) Fritsch.
Mint family   Labiatae

wood edges, meadows
early summer, fall   9-18 in. (2-5 dm)

2-lipped, tubular, stalkless, pink to purple flowers in terminal clusters or in whorls in upper leaf axils. Flowers intermixed with many sharp pointed and densely hairy bracts.

Leaves opposite in pairs, deeply veined, egg-shaped with pointed ends, and hairy. Margins are smooth or shallow toothed.

Stems are hairy, 4-sided, upright; usually only a single stem per plant.

Not the Basil of commerce

MUSK MALLOW
Malva moschata L.
Mallow family   Malvaceae

meadows   summer   1-2 ft. (3-6 dm)

Large (1½-2 in. or 3-5 cm across), pink or white showy flowers; 5 wedge-shaped petals, notched at tips; a central core of bushy, pinkish stamens.

Leaves are palmately compound with (usually) 5 lobes deeply cut almost to the midrib; each lobe is itself deeply cut.

Stem is erect and hairy.

Fruit is a round, fuzzy disk surrounded by the 5 papery calyx lobes.

There are about as many white flower forms as there are pink.

Dame's
Rocket

B

Wild Thyme   D

Honesty

C

Wild
Basil

C

Wild Bergamot   B

Musk Mallow   B

COMMON MILKWEED or Silkweed

Asclepias syriaca L.
Milkweed family   Asclepiadaceae

meadows, dunes summer 2-4 ft. (8-12 dm)

Dusky pink to greenish-purple, fragrant flower clusters are dome or ball-shaped. What appears to be petals are cup-shaped structures, each surrounding a single, curved "horn". The 5 recurved petals (pointing backward along the stem) are immediately below this crown. Below the petals are 5 smaller, greenish sepals.

Leaves are thick, 4-6 in. (10-15 cm) long, softly hairy on the underside, oblong in shape.

Stems are stout and hairy and, when cut or broken, exude a thick, white, milky juice.

Seed pods are long pointed, covered with wart-like bumps. Seeds are tipped with long, silken hairs.

SWAMP MILKWEED

Asclepias incarnata L.
Milkweed family   Asclepiadaceae

wet meadows, swales   summer
3-4 ft. (9-12 dm)

Flowers are pink to purple, rarely white, in umbrella-like clusters at the top of the plant; many flowers on each plant; petals are recurved. Flowers fragrant.

Leaves are smooth and narrow, opposite in pairs.

Stems are stout, smooth to sparsely hairy, and have milky juice.

PLEASE DO NOT PICK

SPREADING DOGBANE

Apocynum androsaemifolium L.
Dogbane family   Apocynaceae

meadows, wood edges   summer
1-4 ft. (3-12 dm)

Usually pink but occasionally nearly white, fragrant flowers, bell-shaped with 5 spreading lobes that have deeper color stripes on their inner side.

Leaves are opposite and paired, smooth, egg-shaped with pointed tips; leafstalks very short; leaf margins smooth.

Stems are reddish and exude a milky juice. Larger stems have fibrous bark.

Fruit is an elongated pod that is round in cross section.

FIREWEED or Great Willow Herb

Epilobium angustifolium L.
Evening Primrose family   Onagraceae

meadows, swales   summer, fall
3-5 ft. (9-15 dm)

Flowers have 4 rounded petals, pink or purplish-pink, form open clusters of conspicuous blossoms. The white stigma at the center of each flower is elongated and terminates in 4 lobes. There are 4 narrow, strap-like sepals between the petals.

Leaves are long, narrow, willow-like, smooth, and alternate.

Stems are erect, smooth, and often reddish color.

TEASEL

Dipsacus sylvestris Huds.
Teasel family   Dipsacaceae

meadows summer, fall 2-6 ft. (6-18 dm)

Flower head composed of many, tiny, tubular, pink, white, or lavender florets interspersed between sharp pointed, slender bracts that are as long or longer than the florets. Immediately below the flower head are numerous, long (up to 4 in. or 1 dm), green, prickly bracts.

Leaves at base of plant are long (often up to 1 ft. or 30 cm or more) and wide (up to 2½ in. or 6 cm). Leaf surfaces are essentially smooth but scattered spines occur on upper leaf surface and the midrib on the under surface has a row of sharp pointed spines. Leaves in pairs with bases that sheath the stem.

Stems are stout, rigidly upright, grooved, densely spiny in upper part.

Seed heads persist through the winter, often used in dried flower arrangements.

FIELD MILKWORT

Polygala sanguinea L.
Milkwort family   Polygalaceae

meadows, swamps   summer
4-16 in. (1-4 dm.)

A tightly packed cluster of rose-purple, white or greenish flowers at tip of stems, forming a short cylindric or round flowerhead.

Leaves are alternate along the stem, simple, stalkless, longer than wide, with entire margins.

Stems are upright, single or branched, densely covered with leaves.

pink and red

Common Milkweed   B

Fireweed

A

Swamp Milkweed   C

Teasel

B

Spreading Dogbane   C

Field Milkwort   C

SMOOTH or Meadow ROSE
Rosa blanda Ait.
Rose family   Rosaceae

wood edges, dunes, meadows
summer   up to 3 ft. (9 dm)

Flowers conspicuous, up to 3 in. (5-7 cm) across, single or in few flowered clusters; 5 pink petals around a central yellow disk supporting numerous stamens.

Leaves are alternate, pinnately compound with 5-7 leaflets each on a short, smooth stalk; leaflets oval to oblong in shape; margins sawtoothed; leafstalks are winged and the stipules at the base of the leafstalks are broadest at their tips.

Upper stems are smooth and essentially thornless; lower stems may have a few slender thorns. A low shrub.

Fruit (hip) is dry, red, smooth, oval and not poisonous.

SWAMP ROSE
Rosa palustris Marsh.
not shown

Flower similar to *R. blanda*. Has many curved thorns; heights to 6 ft. and found in wetter habitats.

MULLEIN-PINK
Lychnis Coronaria (L.) Desr.
Pink family   Caryophyllaceae

meadows   summer   1-3 ft. (3-9 dm)

Flowers have 5 crimson to deep rose color petals (rarely white); one or few flowers per plant. Calyx is tubular, strongly ribbed, and densely covered with long hairs.

Leaves are in pairs with 5-10 pairs along the stem; densely covered with whitish, wool-like hairs. Stems also woolly.

SLEEPY CATCHFLY
Silene antirrhina L.
Pink family   Caryophyllaceae

meadows, dry woods   summer
8-30 in. (2-8 dm.)

Small pink, sometimes white, upright flowers at tip of stem or lateral branches. Petals above an inflated base and do not last. Tips of calyx teeth usually dark red or purple.

Leaves are simple, opposite in pairs, long and narrow, and widely spaced along the stem. Margins are entire.

Stems are upright, minutely hairy at the bottom but smooth at the top. Also near

the top are sticky bands in which insects may be trapped.

CORN COCKLE or Purple Cockle
Agrostemma Githago L.
Pink family   Caryophyllaceae

meadows   summer   1-3 ft. (3-9 dm)

A plant similar to *Lychnis Cornaria* in respect to flower color, number of petals, shape and ribbing of the calyx, and dense hairiness of calyx, leaves, and stems. The most noticeable difference is that this plant has flowers whose 5 calyx lobes greatly exceed the length of the petals, are narrow, and occur between the petals; leaves much narrower.

DEPTFORD PINK
Dianthus Armeria L.
Pink family   Caryophyllaceae

meadows summer up to 20 in. (5 dm)

Pink to red flowers at tip of stems, up to ½ in. (1.25 cm) across.

5 wedge-shaped petals, white spotted, with rounded notches at tips.

Calyx is white-striped, long and fuzzy. Narrow, pointed bracts arise from the base of the calyx and are at least as long as the calyx tube.

Leaves are narrow, linear, 1-2 in. (2.5-5 cm) long and up to ¼ in. (8 mm) wide, in pairs along the stem, and have clasping bases.

Margins are entire but are finely fuzzy.

Stem is mostly smooth but there is some hairiness at leaf joints.

BOUNCING BET or Soapwort
Saponaria officinalis L.
Pink family   Caryophyllaceae

meadows   summer, early fall
1-2 ft. (3-6 dm)

Open clusters of pink, white, or pinkish-white flowers with 5 heart-shaped petals. Base of blossom is a long, greenish tube.

Flowers are fragrant but have an over-all ragged appearance.

Leaves are opposite, 2-3 in. (5-8 cm) long and up to 1 in. (2.5 cm) wide, smooth, have a pointed tip, and veins are parallel.

Stems are coarse, upright, and smooth.

Plants usually found in colonies especially on road shoulders.

pink and red

Corn
Cockle

C

Smooth Rose   C

Mullein-
Pink

C

Deptford Pink   C

Sleepy
Catchfly

C

Bouncing
Bet

B

BULL THISTLE
Cirsium vulgare (Savi) Tenore
Composite family   Compositae

meadows   summer, fall   up to 7 ft. (2 m)

Flower heads mostly single but may be as many as 3 at top of the stem; pink to reddish purple and with diameters up to 2 in. (5 cm). Stiff, yellow tipped spines cover the flower bracts. Only a few flower heads per plant (compared to Canada Thistle).

Leaves are deeply cut, the lobes coarsely toothed and tipped with a sharp pointed spine; leaf margins edged with shorter, prickly spines.

Leaves "flow" into the stem and are persistently woolly on underside.

Stem is coarse, more or less hairy, and prominently covered with stout, exceedingly prickle-tipped wings.

Plant is more robust in every respect than *C. arvense*.

CANADA THISTLE
Cirsium arvense (L.) Scop.
Composite family   Compositae

meadows, swales   summer, fall
3-5 ft. (9-15 dm)

Flowers are globular or flask-shaped, pink to rose-purple or even white (rare), ½-¾ in. (13-19 mm) across, and fragrant. Many flowers per plant.

Leaves alternate along the stem, are irregularly and deeply lobed and spiny-toothed; often woolly on underside of young leaves but become smooth and green on both surfaces of older leaves.

Stems are erect, grooved, and lack spines.

SPOTTED KNAPWEED or Spotted Star Thistle
Centaurea maculosa Lam.
Composite family   Compositae

meadows summer, fall 1-4 ft. (3-12 dm)

A shaggy blossom resembling Bachelor's Button of the cultivated garden to which it is related. Color is usually pink but may range from white to purple. Flowers are at the tips of the stems. Central part of the blossom consists of many individual, tubular flowers. The underpart of the flower head has overlapping, spiny, black-tipped bracts.

Stem leaves are few, deeply cut into narrow segments, are rough to the touch, and grayish-green in color.

Stems are rough, wiry, and grayish-green.

BROWN KNAPWEED
Centaurea Jacea L.
Composite family   Compositae

meadows summer, fall 2-4 ft. (6-12 dm)

Flower color is pink to rose-purple. Bracts below the flower are light brown and appear to be outlined with a yellow-tan fringe. If bracts are removed from flower head their tips have the appearance of having been irregularly torn rather than spiny-tipped (see Spotted Knapweed).

Leaves are alternate, irregularly and inconspicuously toothed (are not deeply cleft). Upper leaves are sessile (without stalks), lower leaves long-stalked and much larger than upper leaves.

JOE-PYE WEED
Eupatorium maculatum L.
Composite family   Compositae

bogs, swales, stream banks   summer, fall   2-6 ft. (6-18 dm)

Flat-topped clusters of pink to purple flowers with 8-20 or more individual blossoms in each flower head.

Leaves are in whorls of 4-5, long, narrow, pointed at both ends, prominently veined, and with sawtooth margins.

Stem is blotched with purplish areas.

CARDINAL-FLOWER
Lobelia Cardinalis L.
Lobelia family   Lobeliaceae

meadows, swales   summer, early fall
18 in.-5 ft. (4.5-15 dm)

Brilliant scarlet-red flowers on an upright spike, each blossom ¾-2 in. (2-5 cm) long. White forms occur but are very rare.

Leaves are thin, long, narrow, up to 6 in. (15 cm) long and 2 in. (5 cm) wide, with upper leaves much smaller than those lower on the plant. Leaf margins are minutely but visibly toothed.

Stems are upright, usually unbranched and usually smooth but may be slightly hairy.

One of the showiest of wildflowers.

PLEASE DO NOT PICK

pink and red

Bull
Thistle

B

Brown
Knapweed

C

Canada
Thistle

B

Joe Pye Weed

B

Spotted
Knapweed

A

Cardinal-
flower

B

BIRD-FOOT VIOLET
Viola pedata L.
Violet family   Violaceae

dry woods   spring   3-6 in. (8-15 cm)

Lavender to blue flowers, ¾-1½ in. (2-4 cm) across; 5 petals, all beardless, lower one with a white spot at its base; nectar lines on this one petal only. Flowerstalks and leafstalks all come from base of plant. Flower is borne somewhat higher than the leaves.

Leaves are long stalked, deeply cleft into long, linear segments resembling a bird foot.

Often found in small clumps.

**PROTECTED MICHIGAN
WILDFLOWER   DO NOT DISTURB**

WILD GINGER
Asarum canadense L.
Birthwort family   Aristolochiaceae

woods   spring   up to 10 in. (25 cm)

A single purple to red-brown flower, tubular at its base and flaring into 3 sharp pointed lobes that may be somewhat recurved (curving backwards). Flowerstalk is short, stout, and arises from between the 2 leaves. Calyx is hairy. There are no petals.

The 2 leaves are spreading, broadly heart-shaped, smooth on the upper surface but fuzzy on the lower; leafstalks are densely hairy; margins are entire. Contact with the leaves may cause a dermatitis on some susceptible people.

JACK-IN-THE-PULPIT or Indian Turnip
Arisaema triphyllum (L.) Schott.
Arum family   Araceae

swamps, bogs, woods   spring
1-3 ft. (3-9 dm)

Flowers are tiny, inconspicuous, hidden, borne at the base of the club-like "Jack". The canopy over the "Jack", and the "pulpit" are green or brownish-purple, often striped.

Leaves 1-3, usually 2, each divided into 3 leaflets.

Stems are stout, upright, often mottled with purple and green, and have a sheathing membrane at the base.

Fruits are bright red berries in a tight cluster. Poisonous.

PLEASE DO NOT PICK

WOOD PHLOX
Phlox divaricata L.
Phlox family   Polemoniaceae

woods   spring, early summer
10-20 in. (2.5-5 dm)

Lavender to pale blue, pinwheel-like flowers in a cluster radiating from tip of stem. 5 wedge-shaped petals that may be notched at their tips. Stamens hidden within the flower tube. Flowers are ¾-1¼ in. (2-3 cm) across.

Leaves are opposite, long and narrow, downy to somewhat hairy, tips blunt pointed; margins are entire; only a few leaves on a plant.

Stems are somewhat sticky and hairy.

HAIRY VETCH
Vicia villosa Roth.
Bean family   Fabaceae

meadows   late spring, summer
2-3 ft. (6-9 dm)

Tightly packed clusters of miniature pea flowers strung along one side of the flowering spike; color is lavender to blue-violet or blue; bicolored.

Leaves are pinnately compound with 10-20 fuzzy leaflets; the central fuzzy leafstalk terminates in a thread-like tendril which may be branched. A pair of stipules (miniature leaves) are at the base of the leafstalk, are hairy, and the shape of half an arrowhead. Stems are upright to reclining (mostly the latter) and are fuzzy.

Fruit is an elongated, flat pod.

BLUE COHOSH or Papoose-root
Caulophyllum thalictroides (L.) Michx.
Barberry family   Berberidaceae

woods   late spring   1-3 ft. (3-9 dm)

Flowers have 6 sharp pointed sepals that resemble petals and may be purple, brown, yellow-green, or greenish-yellow. The 6 petals are much smaller, are various shades of yellow, are found at the base of the sepals, and are hood-shaped. Each flower is up to ½ in. (1.3 cm) across and forms loose, terminal clusters.

Leaves are pinnately compound, 2 or 3 times subdivided; leaflets 2-5 with wedge-shaped bases and usually 3 (sometimes 5) pointed lobes. Leaflets resemble those of Meadow rue. Fruit is a cluster of paired, blue berry-like seeds. All parts poisonous to eat.

Bird-foot
Violet

C

Wood
Phlox

B

Wild
Ginger

D

Hairy
Vetch

B

Jack-in-the-
pulpit

D

Blue
Cohosh

D

VIRGINIA WATERLEAF
Hydrophyllum virginianum L.
Waterleaf family   Hydrophyllaceae

woods, swales   early summer   1-3 ft. (3-9 dm)

Open clusters of pale lavender to white flowers on long stalks usually well above the leaves. Each flower is funnel or bell-shaped with 5 stamens projecting well beyond the petals. Sepals are bristly.

Leaves are stalked, very deeply cut, almost to the midrib to form 5 lobes which are sharp pointed and coarsely toothed. Leaves often have blotchy white markings resembling water marks.

Stem is smooth and weak.

HOUND'S TONGUE
Cynoglossum officinale L.
Borage family   Boraginaceae

meadows, dunes   early summer 1-3 ft. (3-9 dm)

Reddish-purple or dull red flowers, nodding, bell-shaped with 5 rounded lobes, ⅜ in. (1 cm) across. Flowerstalks continue to elongate during flowering reaching lengths of up to 8 in. (2 dm).

Lower leaves up to 12 in. (3 dm) long including the long, winged, leafstalk. Upper leaves progressively smaller than lower and shorter-stalked, ultimately stalkless. Leaves and stems velvety fuzzy. In fruit the 5 fuzzy calyx scales form a perfect star, cupping 4 flattened nutlets covered with hooked spines. Cling to clothing.

BUTTERWORT
Pinguicula vulgaris L.
Bladderwort family   Lentibulariaceae

bogs, shores, wet areas   early summer up to 8 in. (20 cm)

Flowers are pale lavender to reddish-purple, 5 petals and a spur, solitary at tip of flowerstalk. Somewhat resembles a violet (Viola) flower.

Leaves are distinctive, all basal, light yellow-green, greasy, edges rolled inward. Slimy substance coats leaves which traps insects that are then digested by the plant.

STRIPED CORALROOT
Corallorhiza striata Lindl.
Orchid family   Orchidaceae

woods   spring, early summer up to 16 in. (4 dm)

Purple to reddish striped flowers in a spike of 10-20 blossoms. Individual flowers are drooping and up to 1¼ in. (31 mm) long. Plant appears to be leafless but 3-4 scale-like bracts can be found near the base of the stem. Plant is a saprophyte lacking chlorophyll so stems are various shades of purple, brown, or yellow rather than green. Often found in clumps.

SPOTTED CORALROOT
Corallorhiza maculata Raf.
Orchid family   Orchidaceae

woods   summer   up to 20 in. (5 dm)

Similar to above but flowers are spotted rather than striped, blooms a bit later in the season, usually taller, often more flowers per spike (10-40) but these are smaller (up to ¾ in. or 2 cm long.)

NORTHERN or Early CORALROOT
Corallorhiza trifida Chat.
not shown

In contrast to the above species the flowers are white to yellow-green. Lip may be purple spotted. Blooms earlier (May) and is a smaller plant up to 12 in. or 30 cm. Stems are yellowish.

SELF-HEAL or Heal-All
Prunella vulgaris L.
Mint family   Labiatae

meadows, lawns   spring through fall up to 12 in. (3 dm)

Flowers are 2-lipped, the upper lip hood-shaped and erect, the lower divided into 3 lobes, the 2 side lobes smaller than the central lobe which is also fringed. Color is variable being lavender, blue, pink, or white. Flowers arise from between green, leafy bracts which are closely packed together to form a dense, often 4-sided column terminating the stem.

Leaves are opposite, elongate-oval, with margins that are entire to finely toothed.

Stems 4-sided, hairy to slightly fuzzy, erect or often reclining along the ground.

Virginia
Waterleaf

C

Striped
Coralroot

C

Hound's
Tongue

C

Spotted
Coralroot

C

Butterwort

C

Self-heal

C

LARGE-LEAVED ASTER
Aster macrophyllus L.
Composite family   Compositae

woods, wood edges   late summer
1-4 ft. (3-12 dm)

Open clusters of pale lavender, violet, or white flowers at top of plant. Rays ("petals") 9-20 in number, from a central yellow disk that becomes reddish with age.

Lower leaves are long-stalked, large (4-8 in. or 10-20 cm wide), decreasing in size up the stem, surfaces rough to touch, margins with sawtooth edges. Upper leaves are stalkless.

There are large colonies of sterile (flowerless) plants consisting of the large, heart-shaped leaves while the flowering plants are few and scattered.

SMOOTH ASTER
Aster laevis L.
Composite family   Compositae

meadows, dunes   late summer, fall
1-3 ft. (3-9 dm)

Flowers are showy and conspicuous, many per plant. Each flower has 15-20 "petals" which may be lavender, pale violet, blue, or white. Center of flower is yellow, becoming darker and even reddish as the flower ages.

Leaves are thick, variable in size and shape but longer than broad. Those on upper stem become smaller, in fact, so small as to be mere bracts. Margins of upper leaves are entire, lower leaf margins sawtoothed. All leaf edges minutely hairy. Leaf bases clasp the stem. Stem and leaf surfaces are smooth.

NEW ENGLAND ASTER
Aster novae-angliae L.
Composite family   Compositae

meadows   late summer, fall
3-7 ft. (9-21 dm)

The lavender to purple flowers are extremely showy because of their size (1-2 in. or 2.5-5 cm) and the vibrant color. There are from 45 to 100 "petals". The flower head is somewhat sticky.

Leaves and stem are conspicuously hairy.

Note: This aster prefers a moister habitat than *A. laevis* and the flowers are larger (flowers of Smooth Aster seldom larger than ¾ in. or 2 cm across).

ROUGH BLAZING STAR
Liatris aspera Michx.
Composite family   Compositae

meadows   late summer
2-4 ft. (6-12 dm)

Many clusters of lavender to pink flower heads on a spike, short-stalked or stalkless from leaf axils. Ragged or feathery appearance is due to the projecting stamens.

Lower leaves are long, up to 14 in. (35 cm) counting the leafstalk, and up to 1¾ in. (4.5 cm) wide. Size decreases toward top of plant where leaves become sessil (stalkless). All leaves are thick, have smooth edges, and covered with minute, white dots. Usually one stem covered with fine fuzz and bearing many leaves.

COMMON BURDOCK
Arctium minus Schk.
Composite family   Compositae

meadows   summer, fall   2-6 ft. (6-18 dm)

Purplish to pink tubular florets atop a green, spiny burr, ½-1 in. (12-25 mm) wide which is stalkless or short stalked from upper leaf axils.

Upper leaves are heart-shaped but without indentation, lower leaves larger than upper, leaves up to 1 ft. (30 cm) long or more are common; leafstalks are hollow; margins are wavy and minutely toothed.

The hooked barbs on the burs cling to clothing. GREAT BURDOCK, Arctium Lappa L. (not shown) is a larger, more robust plant in all respects. The flowerstalks are longer, flowerheads larger, and plant it taller, up to 8 ft. (24 dm.).

TICK-TREFOIL, POINTED LEAVED
Desmodium glutinosum (Muhl.) Wood
Bean family   Fabaceae

dry woods   summer   1-4 ft. (3-12 dm.)

Purple to pink pea-like flowers rather sparsely spaced along a single or many branched, hairy flowerstalk.

Leaves are compound with 3 leaflets; the 2 lateral leaflets are short-stalked or sessile, the terminal leaflet longer stalked and more sharply pointed. Blades about as broad as long. Leaves form a whorl from which the central flowerstalk arises.

Stem is erect and hairy.

Fruits are flat, 3 jointed, roughly triangular pods covered with hooked hairs that cling to clothing.

lavender and purple

Large-leaved
Aster

C

Rough
Blazing Star

B

Smooth
Aster

B

Common Burdock   C

New England
Aster

B

Tick-Trefoil

C

95

MARSH THISTLE
Cirsium palustre (L.) Scop.
Composite family   Compositae

meadows, swales summer 1-7 ft. (3-20 dm)

Flower heads about ¾ in. (2 cm) across, uniformly purple, found in tight clusters at tip of stem; bracts are compressed against the flower head (not spreading) purple in color especially as maturity advances, are not spiny tipped, have a cobwebby appearance most noticeable just below the bracts.

Leaves are deeply cleft, strongly spiny, downy, webbed with hairs, and mostly on lower part of plant. Leaves on upper stem are fewer, smaller, and simpler. Stem is spiny winged and hollow; stiffly upright.

MARSH CINQUEFOIL
Potentilla palustris (L.) Scop.
Rose family   Rosaceae

swamps, bogs, meadows   summer
1-2 ft. (3-6 dm)

The purple flowers are made of 2 rings of petal-like structures. The true petals are smaller and immediately below them is a ring of larger (broader and longer) petal-like sepals. Flowers are about 1 in. (2.5 cm) across.

Leaves palmately compound with 5-7 leaflets; each leaflet is long and narrow and toothed along the margin.

Stems are hairy, stout, and upright.

HAIRY BEARD-TONGUE
Penstemon hirsutus (L.) Willd.
Snapdragon family   Scrophulariaceae

meadows, open woods   summer
up to 3 ft. (1 m).

Tubular flowers up to 1 in. (2.5 cm) long, pale lavender with whitish tips, borne on long, hairy flowerstalks at tip of plant. One stamen is prominently yellow-bearded.

Leaves are simple, opposite, stalkless, long and narrow, and have sawtooth margins.

Stems are densely hairy, stiffly upright, usually purplish at the base, and often several per plant.

PURPLE LOOSESTRIFE or
Spiked Loosestrife
Lythrum Salicaria L.
Loosestrife family   Lythraceae

swales, swamps   summer, fall
2-5 ft. (6-15 dm)

Reddish-purple flowers borne close together in a terminal spike; each flower has 6 petals but some may be found with 4, 5, or 7. Leaves are narrow, long, up to 4 in. (10 cm), and usually opposite each other but occasionally may be single or in 3's.

Stems are stout, upright, ridged, usually smooth but may be somewhat fuzzy.

Plants occur in colonies, often covering sizable areas with their characteristic color.

NIGHTSHADE
Solanum Dulcamara L.
Nightshade family   Solanaceae

swales   summer, fall
2-12 ft. (6 dm-4 m)

Flowers with 5 purple to blue swept-back petals. There is a protruding yellow cone from the center of the blossom.

Leaves usually with 3 lobes, the oval shaped central lobe being large (1½-4 in. or 4-10 cm long) with 2 much smaller lobes at the base of the leaf. The 2 smaller lobes may be absent from leaves on the lower stem.

Stems are woody at their base; hairy, weak, and twining in upper portion. Vines may climb to heights of up to 12 feet (4 m).

Fruit is an egg-shaped berry that hangs in clusters; red when ripe. The immature (green) berries and the foliage are poisonous. It is claimed that the ripe red berries are non-toxic, have been used in cooking, but eating raw cannot be recommended.

SQUARE-STEMMED MONKEY FLOWER
Mimulus ringens L.
Figwort family   Scrophulariaceae

wet areas   summer, early fall
up to 3 ft. (1 m)

Flowers are blue or, sometimes, violet, pink or white; about 1 in. (2.5-3 cm) long, solitary, on separate flowerstalks which are approximately double the length of the flower and are opposite in pairs from leaf axils.

Leaves are opposite, long and narrow, stalkless, and have sawtooth margins.

Stems are 4-sided and smooth.

Marsh
Thistle

B

Purple Loosestrife   A

Marsh
Cinquefoil

C

Nightshade

C

Hairy Beard-tongue   C

Square-stemmed Monkey Flower   C

97

PURPLE FRINGED ORCHID
Habenaria psycodes (L.) Spreng.
Orchid family   Orchidaceae

swamps, meadows   summer
1-3 ft. (3-9 dm)

Flower head is a spike of fragrant, magenta, pink, or light blue (rarely white) blossoms numbering up to 80 per spike; lower lip of each blossom is deeply cut into 3 fan-shaped segments, each of which is definitely fringed along its edge. Spike is up to 2 in. (5 cm) in diameter and 8 in. (20 cm) in length.

Lower leaves are broad, parallel veined, and bases clasp the stem; upper leaves are much smaller.

PROTECTED MICHIGAN WILDFLOWER
DO NOT DISTURB

MOTHERWORT
Leonurus Cardiaca L.
Mint family   Labiatae

wood edges   summer
to 5 ft. (15 dm)

Flowers small, 2-lipped from a tubular base, upper lip arched, lower with 3 lobes; interior of petals lavender to purple spotted or solid. Outside of upper lip is densely, white-hairy. Flowers form whorls in leaf axils.

Leaves are in pairs, long stalked. Lower leaves with 3, long, sharp pointed lobes at terminal end, each with a few sharp teeth; upper leaves simpler, smaller.

Stem is erect, stout, 4-sided, hairy on the upper part but smooth on lower portion.

SPEARMINT
Mentha spicata L.
Mint family   Labiatae

swales, meadows   summer, fall
8-20 in. (2-5 dm)

Pale lavender to pink, tubed flowers with protruding stamens. Tiny individual blossoms in long, thin spikes at tips of the uppermost branches, formed in whorls in leaf axils (leaf size is greatly reduced in the blossom area). There is a short gap between clusters.

Leaves are in pairs and either stalkless or have very short stalks (3 mm or less); leaves are smooth, prominently veined; margins are toothed. Crushed leaves have a strong odor and taste of spearmint.

Stems are 4-sided and quite smooth.

WILD MINT
Mentha arvensis L.
Mint family   Labiatae

meadows   summer, early fall
6-24 in. (1.5-6 dm)

Individual flowers are similar to preceding species. However, the clusters are spaced out along the stem in the leaf axils with a wide gap between clusters. Leaf size in the blossom area is not reduced. Flower color ranges from pale violet to lavender and (rarely) white.

Leaves are also similar to other two species and have a strong minty taste and odor.

Stem is fuzzy to hairy, 4-sided.

PEPPERMINT
Mentha piperita L.
Mint family   Labiatae

meadows, streambanks   summer, early fall   1-3 ft. (3-9 dm)

Individual flowers similar to *M. spicata*. Flower spikes are thicker, shorter, and gaps between clusters much reduced.

Leaves are also similar, in pairs, have toothed margins, but the leafstalks are longer (4-15 mm) especially on larger leaves. Crushed leaves have a strong peppermint taste and odor.

Stems are smooth, 4-sided, and tend to be purple in color.

BLUE-EYED MARY
Collinsia verna Nutt.
Figwort family   Scrophulariaceae

woods, swales   spring   8-16 in. (2-4 dm.)

Bicolored flowers with a white upper lip and bright blue lower. 5 petals notched at tips; appear as 4 with a 5th petal folded lengthwise and hidden between the other 2 blue petals.

Lower leaves are broad to nearly round on long leafstalks. Upper leaves mostly long, narrow, stalkless, and in opposite pairs or in whorls. Margins coarsely toothed to entire.

Stems are single or many, smooth below and slightly hairy above; weak with many tending to recline.

This species not widely distributed but where found forms brilliant, showy colonies, especially on wooded, riverbottom soils.

Purple
Fringed Orchid

C

Wild
Mint

D

Peppermint

C

Motherwort   D

Spearmint

C

Blue-Eyed Mary   C

LUPINE
Lupinus perennis L.
Bean family   Fabaceae

meadows   spring, early summer
1-2 ft. (3-6 dm)

Blue, blue-violet, pink, or white pea flowers on short stalks from the central stem forming an open spike of blossoms; spike up to 10 in. (25 cm) long at tip of stem above the leaves.

Leaves are palmately compound with 7-11 leaflets, each 1-2 in. (2-5 cm) long.

Stems are erect, fuzzy, usually many branched.

Fruit is a hairy, elongated pod.

GARDEN LUPINE
Lupinus polyphyllus Lindl.
Bean family   Fabaceae

meadows   summer   2-4 ft. (6-12 dm)

Extremely showy spikes of blue, violet, pink, or white, large, pea flowers closely packed along a central stem at top of plant; flower spike is up to 18 in. (46 cm) long.

Leaves are palmately compound with 12-18 leaflets.

A garden escape, larger and showier than *L. perennis*. Found primarily in the Keweenaw Peninsula and southward into the western counties of the Upper Peninsula.

COMMON BLUE VIOLET
Viola papilionacea Pursh.
Violet family   Violaceae

woods, meadows spring 3-8 in. (8-20 cm)

The 5-petaled flowers are blue to light or dark purple, the lower petal smooth and extending backwards into a short spur; the 2 side petals are bearded, and all 3 have strongly contrasting color veins (nectar lines).

Leaves are broadly heart-shaped with coarse, round toothed margins; smooth leafstalks may be up to 5 in. (13 cm) long.

This is one of the "stemless" violet group with both the leafstalks and flowerstalks arising from a buried rhizome or underground stem.

Violets hybridize freely causing countless variations.

BLUE IRIS or Blue Flag
Iris versicolor L.
Iris family   Iridaceae

swales, swamps   late spring, early summer   2-3 ft. (6-9 dm)

Blossoms consist of petals and sepals that are both of the same general color, sepals are widespreading and marked at the base with a greenish-yellow or yellow blotch; petals stand upright, are ½-⅔ the length of the sepals. Both the petals and the sepals are strongly marked with darker colored veins.

Leaves are long and narrow resembling the blade of a sword, arise mainly from the base of the plant.

DWARF LAKE IRIS
Iris lacustris Nutt.
Iris family   Iridaceae

beaches, bogs   late spring
less than 8 in. (2 dm)

Structure of flower is similar to *I. versicolor*. Flower is about 2″ (5 cm) across.

Leaves are flat, ½ in. (1.3 cm) broad and 3-6 in. (8-15 cm) long at blossom time but later grow to a length of up to 8 in. (20 cm). This is a miniature iris plant found almost exclusively on the sandy or gravelly shores of Lakes Michigan, and Huron and in marshy or boggy areas adjacent.

Usually found in colonies.

A THREATENED SPECIES
DO NOT DISTURB

BLUE-EYED GRASS
Sisyrinchium albidum Raf.
Iris family   Iridaceae

meadows, swales   spring
6-18 in. (1.5-4.5 dm)

The "eye" of blue-eyed grass is yellow (the center of the flower where the base of the blue, lavender, or white petals and sepals change to yellow). The 3 petals and 3 sepals are identical in appearance and each sharply pointed at its tip. The flower is exceeded by a sharp pointed bract that terminates the stem.

Leaves are flat, narrow (3 mm), grasslike, arise from base of plant, sharply folded at the base, and pointed at tips.

Stems are stiff, erect, winged on 2 sides making stem appear flat.

blue

Lupine

B

Blue Iris   B

Garden
Lupine

B

Dwarf Lake Iris   C

Blue-
Eyed grass

D

Common Blue Violet   C

HAREBELL or Bluebell
Campanula rotundifolia L.
Harebell family   Campanulaceae

dunes, meadows   spring, summer
12-18 in. (3-4.5 dm)

Bell-shaped flowers with 5-pointed lobes, nodding at the end of thin, wiry stems. Color is usually blue but may be pink or white.

Basal leaves are long-stalked, roundish, and tend to dry up and disappear before the flowers appear. Stem leaves are long and narrow, up to 4 in. (10 cm) in length.

PERIWINKLE or Myrtle
Vinca minor L.
Dogbane family   Apocynaceae

woods   spring, summer   *see below

A 5-petaled blue flower up to 1 in. (2.5 cm) across, on short, erect stemlets, rising above the uppermost 2 pair of leaves. A white, 5-pointed star is out-lined in the center of the blossom. Petals are blunt tipped.

Leathery, shiny leaves in pairs along the stem remain green year around.

*Smooth stems recline along the ground, vine-like, up to 3 ft. (1 m) long, forming mats that may cover large areas. This plant is a garden escape and often found in the vicinity of old or abandoned homesteads, cemeteries, and along roadsides.

COMMON SPEEDWELL
Veronica officinalis L.
Figwort family   Scrophulariaceae

woods, meadows, lawns
spring to fall   prostrate

4-petaled pale blue or lavender flowers. There are 3 spreading, somewhat rounded petals, the 4th petal being dis-tinctly smaller; a pair of projecting stamens. Flowers ¼ in. (6 mm) across, sparsely distributed along an upturned flowerstalk that arises from the prostrate, hairy stem.

Leaves mostly oval with a wedge-shaped base, up to 2 in. (5 cm) long; margins are sharp toothed.

Stems root from the nodes.

FORGET-ME-NOT
Myosotis scorpioides L.
Borage family   Boraginaceae

swamps, moist areas   spring to fall
6-24 in. (1.5-6 dm)

Flowers are small, up to ¼ in. (6 mm) across, very pale blue or white (rarely pink); 5 rounded petals; center of flower is yellow with 5 star-like points. The stemlets bearing the flowers tend to uncoil as the blossoms open.

Leaves are stalkless, longer than broad, hairy, and alternate along the stem.

Stems are hairy, upright in young plants but later are more or less prostrate along the ground.

Usually in colonies forming a showy mat of blossoms.

BLUEWEED or Viper's Bugloss
Echium vulgare L.
Borage family   Boraginaceae

meadows   summer, early fall
2-3 ft. (6-9 dm)

Bright blue to violet-blue flowers on short, curved stalks from the main stem. Prominent, long red stamens project beyond the petals. Flower buds are pink. Flowers are sometimes white or pink.

Leaves are long, narrow, and very hairy on both surfaces so leaves feel velvety.

Stems have many, small, brownish dots from which bristly spines arise. Entire plant is conspicuously bristly-hairy.

PICKERELWEED
Pontederia cordata L.
Pickerelweed family   Pontederiaceae

shallow water, ponds   summer, fall
1-3 ft. (3-9 dm)*

Tiny blue flowers on narrow spikes, the flowering portion being up to 4 in. (10 cm) long. Each flower is 2-lipped with each lip 3-lobed.

Leaves are smooth, broad, heart-shaped; with a deep indentation at the base.

Plants grow partially submerged in shal-low water, usually in colonies

*This is the height above the surface of the water.

blue

Harebell   C

Forget-me-not   C

Periwinkle   C

Blueweed

B

Common Speedwell   D

Pickerelweed   C

CHICORY or Blue Sailors
Cichorium Intybus L.
Composite family   Compositae

meadows summer, fall up to 5 ft. (15 dm)

Showy flowers that are almost always blue but in rare cases might be white or pink. Petals are blunt and fringed at the tip.

Blossoms are stalkless, attached directly to the main stem.

The basal leaves are dandelion-like, the margins having jagged, sharp pointed lobes. Leaves on the stem are few and small, especially on the upper stem. Upper and lower leaf surfaces are hairy and long hairy on the lower side of the midrib. Stem leaves clasp the stem with sharp pointed projections.

Stems are wiry, tough, shallow grooved, and sparsely to densely covered with weak spines.

COMMON SKULLCAP or Marsh Skullcap
Scutellaria galericulata L.
Mint family   Labiatae

swamps, shores, meadows   summer, fall   up to 30 in. (7.6 dm)

Blue, violet-blue, pink, or white flowers borne singly or in pairs in leaf axils, ¾-1 in. (2-2.5 cm) in length on very short flower-stalks; tubular at base flaring into 2 lips, the upper one of which is hooded forming the "skullcap".

Leaves are opposite in pairs, very short stalked or stalkless, long, narrow with pointed tips; margins slightly toothed; lower leaf surface often fuzzy, upper surface less so.

Stems square in cross section, erect, hairy.

BLUE VERVAIN
Verbena hastata L.
Vervain family   Verbenaceae

meadows, swales, marshes   summer, early fall   18 in-5 ft. (4.5-15 dm)

The single stem terminates in a many branched flower head of individual spikes, each spike bearing a cluster of small, blue to violet-blue colored flowers, each with 5 petals. Flowering commences at the base of each spike and progresses upward.

Leaves are opposite, long, narrow, pointed, and toothed along the margins.

Stems are 4-sided, erect, and covered with short hairs.

GREAT LOBELIA
Lobelia siphilitica L.
Lobelia family   Lobeliaceae

meadows, swamps, shores   late summer, fall   1-3 ft. (3-9 dm)

Blue, tubular flowers flaring into 2 lobes at top of blossom and 3 wider lobes at the bottom. Lower lobes are streaked with white.

Flowers are up to 1 in. (2.5 cm) long, borne singly on short spikelets; the several individual flowers together form a wide, conspicuous spike.

Leaves are thin, long, 3-5 in. (8-13 cm) narrow, stalkless, and have finely toothed margins.

Stems are stout, erect, smooth or very slightly hairy.

PLEASE DO NOT PICK

FRINGED GENTIAN
Gentiana crinita Froel.
Gentian family   Gentianaceae

woods, meadows, swales   late summer, fall   1-3 ft. (3-9 dm)

Showy, bright blue or violet (rarely white) flowers with 4 conspicuously fringed petals which arise from a tubed base. A single flower surmounts each stem. Blossoms tend to close at evening and on cloudy days.

Leaves are paired, stalkless, smooth margined, and smaller than Closed Gentian.

**PROTECTED MICHIGAN WILDFLOWER
DO NOT DISTURB**

CLOSED GENTIAN or Bottle Gentian
Gentiana Andrewsii Griseb.
Gentian family   Gentianaceae

woods, meadows, swales   late summer, fall   18 in-3 ft. (4.5-9 dm)

Flowers are blue, violet, or white in upright clusters of egg-shaped blossoms at tip of stem or in upper leaf axils. Blossoms remain closed or nearly so and are tipped with a minute, whitish fringe.

Leaves are in pairs, opposite, stalkless, and have smooth margins; are 1½ in. (4 cm) in width and up to 6 in. (15 cm) long; veins parallel.

**PROTECTED MICHIGAN WILDFLOWER
DO NOT DISTURB**

blue

Great
Lobelia

C

Chicory   B

Common
Skullcap

D

Fringed Gentian   C

Blue
Vervain

B

Closed Gentian   C

SKUNK CABBAGE
Symplocarpus foetidus (L.) Nutt.
Arum family   Araceae

swamps, springy areas   early spring
up to 5 in. (13 cm)*

The stemless flower structure is at
ground level. A shell-like, mottled hood
in colors of green to purple or purple-
brown, up to 5 in. (13 cm) tall, with
rolled edges. The knob in the center of
this shelter bears the tiny, yellow flowers.

At blossom time leaf development is
just beginning and may not yet be visible
or may be tightly inrolled around the
flower structure. *Later in the season
the leaves become very large, up to 2 ft.
(6 dm) long, and broad, somewhat heart-
shaped, and have leafstalks that are
green, grooved, and succulent; margins
smooth to wavy.

SEASIDE ARROW-GRASS
Triglochin maritima L.
Arrow-grass family   Juncaginaceae

shores, bogs, swamps   spring
up to 30 in. (7.5 dm)

Tiny greenish flowers on a very narrow
spike on upper half of flowerstalk, often
many flowerstalks per plant.
Flowerstalks and leaves arise separately
from ground level.

Leaves all basal, upright, grass-like,
fleshy, shorter than the flowering spike.

COMMON CAT-TAIL
Typha latifolia L.
Cat-tail family   Typhaceae

wet open areas   spring, summer
3-9 ft. (1-3 m.)

Hundreds of tiny, brown flowers without
petals or sepals, so closely crowded
together as to form a compact mass resembling a hot dog at the tip of the stem.
The female flowers are separate from the
male flowers, being at the bottom of the
spike, the male flowers just above. There
is no gap (or possibly a very slight one)
between the two sexes.

Leaves are sword-like, ½ in. or more
wide (1.27 cm.), are flat with leaf bases
clasping the stem.

The related NARROW-LEAVED CAT-
TAIL, T. angustifolia L. (not shown) is
not as tall, flower spikes are thinner,
leaves narrower, (not exceeding ½ in. in

width) and there is usually a definite
gap between the male and female flowers.

SPURRED GENTIAN
Halenia deflexa (Sm.) Griseb.
Gentian family   Gentianaceae

bogs, marshes, wet woods   summer
6-30 in. (1.5-8 dm)

4-petaled, greenish, bronze, or purplish
flowers in a cluster at tip of stem or from
upper leaf axils; cone-shaped with 4
projecting spurs from the rear.

Leaves are opposite, oval to elongated
egg-shaped narrowing to pointed tips;
upper leaves stalkless (sessile), lower
with short leafstalks; margins are entire.

Stems are upright, twisted, smooth.

PROTECTED MICHIGAN WILDFLOWER
DO NOT DISTURB

CURLED DOCK or Sour Dock
Rumex crispus L.
Smartweed family   Polygonaceae

meadows   summer, fall
1-4 ft. (3-12 dm)

Small green or reddish-brown, inconspicuous flowers 1-3 mm across, in
whorls on flowerstalks from leaf axils.

Leaves are long, up to 1 ft. (30 cm), and
relatively narrow; strongly veined; wavy
leaf margins.

Stems erect, smooth, ridged, green to
brown. Fruits reddish-brown to brown,
small, 3-winged seeds, only 1-3 mm
across but conspicuous because of their
large numbers and color. Illustration
shows the seeds.

GROUND NUT or Indian Potato
Apios americana Medicus
Bean family   Fabaceae

shores, swales   summer   vine

Brown (also reddish to maroon) color,
fragrant, pea-like flowers form short,
rather dense clusters at end of long
flowerstalks which arise in leaf axils.

Leaves are pinnately compound with 5-7
egg-shaped but sharp pointed leaflets.

Stems are short, climbing vines with
milky juice. Rhizome is thickened at
intervals to form small tubers (resembles
a necklace). Edible.

Skunk
Cabbage

D

Spurred
Gentian

C

Seaside
Arrow-grass

D

Curled
Dock

D

Common
Cat-tail

B

Ground Nut   C

107

HELLEBORINE
Epipactis Helleborine (L.) Crantz.
Orchid family   Orchidaceae

woods   summer   1-3 ft. (3-9 dm)

Terminal spikes of nodding flowers, each with a green calyx tube, ridged and as long as or longer than the purple petals and sepals; each flower from the axil of a long, narrow, leafy bract.

Leaves are alternate, long, narrow, smooth; upper leaves stalkless to very short-stalked while the lower leaves clasp the stem; veins are prominent and parallel; margins entire and finely fuzzy.

Stem is erect, downy, and purplish.

THIS, AND THE NEXT TWO ORCHIDS ARE PROTECTED MICHIGAN WILDFLOWERS DO NOT DISTURB

HEARTLEAF TWAYBLADE
Listera cordata (L.) R.Br.
Orchid family   Orchidaceae

wet woods, bogs, swamps
early summer   3-10 in. (7-25 cm)

Flowers are small (4-5 mm long), strung along an upright spike; green, purplish-green, tan or dark purple; lower lip is longer than the other petals and is forked and spreading.

There is a single pair of heart-shaped, stalkless leaves opposite each other below the middle of the stem.

Stem is smooth except in the area of the flowers.

TALL NORTHERN BOG ORCHID
Habenaria hyperborea (L.) R.Br.
Orchid family   Orchidaceae

bogs, wet woods, swamps   summer
6-40 in. (1.5-10 dm)

Usually dense but sometimes loose spikes of green to yellow-green flowers. Lower lip is relatively long, narrow, and pointed. A projecting spur is about the same length as the lower lip. The green floral bracts are longer than the flowers at the bottom of the spike, but become progressively shorter toward the top.

There are many leaves, some up to 8 in. (20 cm) long. Parallel veined, bases wrapped around the stem; shiny, smooth.

Stem is stout and stiffly upright.

RAGWEED
Ambrosia artemisiifolia L.
Composite family   Compositae

meadows, fields, waste areas
summer, fall   up to 4 ft. (1.2 m.)

The inconspicuous green flowers are either male or female but not both and occur on the same plant. Male flowers are many, borne in spikes at the tips of the stems, are saucer shape, downward facing, and can be loaded with yellow pollen. Female flowers are fewer, occur below the male flowers in the upper leaf axils and forks of branching stems.

Leaves are mostly smooth, deeply cut into many lobes, each lobe, in turn, is deeply cut.

Stems are upright and usually hairy. The pollen from these plants is the primary contributor to the allergy known as hay fever.

TALL WORMWOOD
Artemisia campestris L.
Composite family   Compositae

dunes, dry sand   summer, fall
2-5 ft. (6-15 dm)

Large numbers of tiny, globular, nodding, green to yellow flowers loosely arranged along many short, upward pointing side branches.

Leaves are very finely dissected, almost string-like, aromatic, gray-green.

Usually a single stem plant; stem is smooth.

Somewhat resembles a ragweed and, like it, produces much pollen that is a source of hay fever.

CYPRESS SPURGE
Euphorbia Cyparissias L.
Spurge family   Euphorbiaceae

meadows   spring-summer
8-16 in. (2-4 dm.)

Compare with Leafy Spurge (page 62). There are these differences: (1) In Cypress Spurge bracts of flowerhead, yellowish-green turning to reddish or purplish, are smaller and more broadly rounded. (2) Plants are smaller. (3) Leaves are very narrow and shorter, 1 in. or less (2.5 cm.), even more numerous being really crowded on upper stem.

Like Leafy Spurge the stems are erect and contain milky juice. Plants often form colonies, frequently in or around cemeteries.

Helleborine

D

Ragweed

C

Heartleaf
Twayblade

D

Tall
Wormwood

C

Tall Northern
Bog Orchid

D

Cypress
Spurge

C

OBSERVER'S LIST	seen by			date	location
Agrimony					
Alyssum					
Anemone, Canada					
Anemone, False Rue					
Anemone, Rue					
Anemone, Wood					
Arbutus, Trailing					
Arethusa					
Arrow-grass, Seaside					
Asphodel, Sticky False					
Aster, Flat-topped					
Aster, Large-leaved					
Aster, New England					
Aster, Smooth					
Baneberry, Red					
Baneberry, White					
Basil, Wild					
Bearberry					
Beard-tongue, Hairy					
Bellwort, Large-flowered					
Bergamot, Wild					
Bindweed, Field					
Birdsfoot Trefoil					
Black-eyed Susan					
Blazing Star, Rough					
Bloodroot					
Blue-eyed Grass					
Blue-eyed Mary					
Blueweed					
Boneset					
Bouncing Bet					
Broom-rape, Clustered					
Buckbean					
Bunchberry					
Burdock, Common					
Burdock, Great					
Butter-and-eggs					
Buttercup					
Butterfly Weed					
Butterwort					
Calypso					
Campion, Bladder					
Campion, White					
Cardinal-flower					
Carrot, Wild					
Catnip					
Cat-tail, Common					

Observer's List (cont.)		seen by		date	location
Cat-tail, Narrow-leaved					
Chamomile, Scentless					
Cherry, Ground					
Chicory					
Cinquefoil, Marsh					
Cinquefoil, Sulfur					
Cinquefoil, Three-toothed					
Clintonia					
Clover, Red					
Cockle, Corn					
Cohosh, Blue					
Columbine					
Comandra, Northern					
Coneflower, Tall					
Coralroot, Northern or Early					
Coralroot, Spotted					
Coralroot, Striped					
Coreopsis					
Corydalis, Pale					
Cow Wheat					
Cranberry, Large					
Cranberry, Small					
Cress, Spring					
Cucumber-root, Indian					
Cucumber, Wild					
Culver's Root					
Daisy, Ox-eye					
Dame's Rocket					
Dandelion, Common					
Dock, Curled					
Dogbane, Spreading					
Dogfennel					
Dutchman's Breeches					
Everlasting, Pearly					
Fireweed					
Fleabane					
Foamflower					
Forget-me-not					
Gentian, Closed					
Gentian, Fringed					
Gentian, Spurred					
Geranium, Wild					
Ginger, Wild					
Ginseng, Dwarf					
Goat's-beard					
Goat's-beard					
Goat's-beard, Purple					

Observer's List (cont.)	seen by			date	location
Goat's Rue					
Golden Alexanders					
Goldenrod, Bluestem				.	
Goldenrod, Canada					
Goldthread					
Grass-of-Parnassus					
Grass-of-Parnassus, Small					
Grass Pink					
Greenbrier					
Ground Nut					
Harebell					
Hawkweed, Field or Yellow					
Hawkweed, Orange					
Hawkweed, Smoothish					
Heather, False					
Helleborine					
Hepatica, Round-lobed					
Hepatica, Sharp-lobed					
Herb-Robert					
Honesty					
Horehound, Cut-leaved Water-					
Horsemint					
Hound's Tongue					
Indian Paintbrush					
Indian Pipe					
Indigo, Prairie False					
Iris, Blue					
Iris, Dwarf Lake					
Jack-in-the-pulpit					
Jewelweed, Spotted					
Joe-Pye Weed					
King Devil					
Knapweed, Brown					
Knapweed, Spotted					
Ladies'-tresses, Common					
Lady's-slipper, Pink					
Lady's-slipper, Ram's-head					
Lady's-slipper, Showy					
Lady's-slipper, Yellow					
Lettuce, White					
Lily, Day					
Lily, Dune					
Lily, Fawn					
Lily, Michigan					
Lily-of-the-valley, Wild					
Lily, Yellow Trout					
Lily, Wood					

Observer's List (cont.)	seen by			date	location
Lobelia, Great					
Loosestrife, Purple					
Loosestrife, Tufted					
Lupine					
Lupine, Garden					
Mallow, Musk					
Marigold, Marsh					
May Apple					
Meadow-rue, Early					
Meadow-rue, Purple					
Meadowsweet					
Milkweed, Common					
Milkweed, Swamp					
Milkwort, Field					
Milkwort, Racemed					
Mint, Wild					
Mitrewort					
Mitrewort, Naked					
Moneywort					
Monkey Flower, Square-stemmed					
Motherwort					
Mullein, Common					
Mullein, Moth					
Mullein-pink					
Nightshade					
Nightshade, Enchanters					
Orchid, Purple Fringed					
Orchid, Tall Northern Bog					
Painted Cup, Pale					
Parsnip, Cow					
Parsnip, Water					
Parsnip, Wild					
Partridgeberry					
Pea, Beach					
Pea, Everlasting					
Peppermint					
Periwinkle					
Phlox, Wood					
Pickerelweed					
Pimpernel, Yellow					
Pinesap					
Pink, Deptford					
Pipsissewa					
Pitcher Plant					
Pogonia, Rose					
Poison Ivy					
Polygala, Fringed					

Observer's List (cont.)	seen by			date	location
Pondlily, Yellow					
Primrose, Birdseye					
Primrose, Evening					
Puccoon, Hairy					
Puccoonn, Hoary					
Pyrola, Pink					
Ragweed					
Ragwort, Golden					
Rock Cress, Lyre-leaved					
Rock Sandwort					
Rose, Smooth					
Rose, Swamp					
St. John's-wort, Common					
Sarsaparilla					
Sarsaparilla, Bristly					
Self-heal					
Shinleaf					
Shinleaf, Green					
Showy Orchis					
Silverweed					
Skullcap, Common					
Skunk Cabbage					
Sleepy Catchfly					
Snakeroot, Black					
Snakeroot, White					
Solomon's Seal, False					
Solomon's Seal, Hairy					
Solomon's Seal, Smooth					
Solomon's Seal, Starry False					
Sowthistle, Smooth					
Spearmint					
Speedwell, Common					
Spring Beauty					
Spring Beauty, Broadleaf					
Spurge, Cypress					
Spurge, Flowering					
Spurge, Leafy					
Squawroot					
Squirrel Corn					
Starflower					
Starwort					
Stitchwort, Lesser					
Strawberry, Wild					
Strawberry, Woodland					
Sundew, Round-leaved					
Sunflower, Tall					
Sunflower, Woodland					

Observer's List (cont.)	seen by			date	location
Swamp Candle					
Sweet Cicely					
Tansy, Common					
Tansy, Huron					
Teasel					
Thimbleberry					
Thistle, Bull					
Thistle, Canada					
Thistle, Marsh					
Thistle, Pitcher's					
Thyme, Wild					
Tick-trefoil, Pointed Leaved					
Toadflax, Bastard					
Toothwort, Broadleaf					
Toothwort, Cutleaf					
Trillium					
Trillium, Nodding					
Trillium, Red					
Turtlehead					
Twayblade, Heartleaf					
Twinflower					
Twisted Stalk, Rose					
Twisted Stalk, White					
Vervain, Blue					
Vetch, Crown					
Vetch, Hairy					
Violet, Bird-foot					
Violet, Canada					
Violet, Common Blue					
Violet, Downy Yellow					
Violet, Smooth Yellow					
Virgin's Bower					
Water Arum					
Water Hemlock					
Waterleaf, Virginia					
Water Lily, White					
Windflower, Red					
Wintergreen					
Woodnymph					
Wood-sorrel, Yellow					
Wormwood, Tall					
Yarrow					
Yellow Rocket					

Index